EMOTIONAL
INTELLIGENCE POCKETBOOK

EMOTIONAL INTELLIGENCE POCKETBOOK

LITTLE EXERCISES FOR AN INTUITIVE LIFE

Gill Hasson

CAPSTONE
A Wiley Brand

This edition first published 2017

© 2017 Gill Hasson

Registered office

John Wiley & Sons Ltd, The Atrium, Southern Gate, Chichester, West Sussex, PO19 8SQ, United Kingdom

For details of our global editorial offices, for customer services and for information about how to apply for permission to reuse the copyright material in this book, please see our website at www.wiley.com.

The right of the author to be identified as the author of this work has been asserted in accordance with the Copyright, Designs and Patents Act 1988.

All rights reserved. No part of this publication may be reproduced, stored in a retrieval system, or transmitted, in any form or by any means, electronic, mechanical, photocopying, recording or otherwise, except as permitted by the UK Copyright, Designs and Patents Act 1988, without the prior permission of the publisher.

Wiley publishes in a variety of print and electronic formats and by print-on-demand. Some material included with standard print versions of this book may not be included in e-books or in print-on-demand. If this book refers to media such as a CD or DVD that is not included in the version you purchased, you may download this material at http://booksupport.wiley.com. For more information about Wiley products, visit www.wiley.com.

Designations used by companies to distinguish their products are often claimed as trademarks. All brand names and product names used in this book are trade names, service marks, trademarks or registered trademarks of their respective owners. The publisher is not associated with any product or vendor mentioned in this book.

Limit of Liability/Disclaimer of Warranty: While the publisher and author have used their best efforts in preparing this book, they make no representations or warranties with respect to the accuracy or completeness of the contents of this book and specifically disclaim any implied warranties of merchantability or fitness for a particular purpose. It is sold on the understanding that the publisher is not engaged in rendering professional services and neither the publisher nor the author shall be liable for damages arising herefrom. If professional advice or other expert assistance is required, the services of a competent professional should be sought.

Library of Congress Cataloging-in-Publication Data is available

A catalogue record for this book is available from the British Library.

ISBN 978-0-857-08730-0 (pbk) ISBN 978-0-857-08729-4 (ebk)
ISBN 978-0-857-08732-4 (ebk)

10 9 8 7 6 5 4 3 2 1

Cover Design and Illustration: Wiley

Set in 10/12.5pt RotisSansSerifStd by Aptara Inc., New Delhi, India

Printed in Great Britain by TJ International Ltd, Padstow, Cornwall, UK

CONTENTS

INTRODUCTION

It is very important to understand that emotional intelligence is not the opposite of intelligence, it is not the triumph of head over heart – it is the unique intersection of both. – David Caruso

What's emotional intelligence about? Emotional intelligence is about using your emotions to inform your thinking and using your thinking to understand and manage your emotions.

For many of us, with so many competing demands, concerns and commitments in our lives, it's easy to feel overwhelmed and stressed, to become unsure and confused, to misunderstand or be misunderstood by others.

With emotional intelligence, by understanding your emotions and how to manage them, you're better able to express how you feel, what you want and don't want, while at the same time acknowledging and understanding how others are feeling and behaving.

It's a dynamic process; the extent to which you can understand and manage your own emotions influences your ability to understand and manage other people's emotions. And the more you understand other people's emotions, their intentions, motivations and behaviour, the more appropriately you can respond and the more effectively you can interact with them.

Emotional intelligence can help you to live and work with others more easily; forge stronger relationships, both in your personal life and at work. You're more able to sense and manage the emotional needs of others. You're more able to think before responding and know to give yourself and others time to calm down if emotions become overwhelming.

Developing your emotional intelligence can help you to lead a happier life because thinking and behaving rationally and calmly in difficult situations puts you in a better position to handle feelings and situations that you may have found difficult and challenging in the past.

But emotional intelligence is not only about understanding and managing *difficult* situations and emotions. It's also about knowing how to engage the 'feel good' emotions that can give you and other people positivity, confidence, support, motivation and inspiration.

HOW TO USE THIS BOOK

Life will continue to throw us the same lessons until we learn from them. – Rachel Woods

There are four parts to this book:

1. Understanding emotions.
2. Managing emotions.
3. Developing your emotional intelligence.
4. Developing your social intelligence.

Within each part you'll find particular situations or circumstances and for each situation or circumstance you will find practical ways – ideas, advice, tips and techniques – to help you to understand and apply emotional intelligence.

If you want to understand what emotions are, where they come from and why we have them, read the chapters in Part 1, 'Understanding emotions'. If you want to develop your emotional intelligence and learn how to manage emotions – yours or other people's – Parts 2, 3 and 4 of this book will help you. Whether you want to learn how to manage difficult emotions such as anger and disappointment, build your courage and confidence or motivate and inspire others, whatever the issue, simply pick out a few ideas, tips and techniques that appeal to you and give them a try.

Some of the tips and advice will be particularly comfortable and helpful to you in certain situations and with particular people. Use them. The more often you use them, the more you'll know that events, feelings, other people and yourself *can* be managed better with emotional intelligence.

If you feel that difficult emotions – stress, sadness, loneliness, guilt, regret, disappointment, anxiety, depression or anger – are overwhelming you and you're really struggling to cope, do turn to the back of this book where you'll find a list of organisations that can give you information and advice online or via their helpline.

But for everyday situations, do keep this book in your bag or your pocket whenever or wherever you need emotional intelligence. You'll find that the tips, techniques, ideas and suggestions in this book really can help provide you with a sense of calm control, perspective and understanding.

PART 1
UNDERSTANDING EMOTIONS

KNOWING WHY
WE HAVE EMOTIONS

Everyone knows what an emotion is until asked to give a definition. Then it seems, nobody knows. – B. Fehr and J. Russell

Emotions play an important role in how we think and behave. Emotions help protect you and keep you physically safe by prompting you to react to the threat of danger. Basic emotions such as fear, anger and disgust don't wait for you to think, to reason and process what's going on. In circumstances where rational thinking is too slow, these emotions instantly warn you of danger and get you to react – through fight or flight – immediately.

Other emotions – social emotions – enable people to live and work with each other. Social emotions such as guilt, shame, gratitude and love guide and maintain interactions and bonds that bring people – families, friends, neighbours and communities – together.

Emotions also allow us to create and express ideas and thoughts that wouldn't necessarily come about through rational thinking. Anger, for example, can inspire a dramatic painting. Despair and sadness can inspire beautiful, moving poetry, songwriting and music. Art, music and literature all provoke and inspire emotions and create an emotional connection between the art, music or writing and the viewer, listener or reader.

Emotions then, all have a positive intent; they help keep you safe, help you establish and maintain connections with others, and inspire creativity. On the one hand, emotions can focus our thoughts and behaviour and on the other hand, can enhance and widen thoughts and experience.

In Practice

Nothing vivifies and nothing kills like the emotions. – Joseph Roux

Be more aware of and develop your understanding of the physical safety and the social and creative purposes of emotions:

- Think of situations when an emotion prompted you to do or say something automatically, without thinking. Where you acted instantly, for example, out of fear, disgust or anger, you responded without thinking.
- Think of times when you've experienced a social emotion; an emotion that has prompted you to do or say something to manage the interactions between you and someone else.

Have there been occasions when, for example, you've tried to put things right because you've felt guilty about a wrongdoing?

- Think of a time when someone else has shown you empathy, compassion or kindness. Did it help you to feel understood, comforted or supported?
- What about the times others' emotions have influenced you? Perhaps you've noticed that someone was frustrated and upset and it prompted you to offer them your help.

Think of the songs and music you like to listen to. How do particular songs or pieces of music make you feel? What music, films, poems, books, paintings inspire you? Which songs and music lift your spirits? What films, music, poems, etc. make you feel sad and reflective?

Over the next few days, notice when your emotions motivate your action, save you time, help you get something done, or help you to reach out and respond to someone else.

UNDERSTANDING THE ASPECTS OF EMOTIONS

Emotions bridge thought, feeling, and action. – John D. Mayer

Whether you're aware of it or not, when you experience an emotion, it is made up of three aspects: thoughts, physical feelings and behaviour.

There's no one specific order in which the aspects of an emotion occur, but any one aspect can affect the others. What you think can affect how you feel physically. It can also alter how you behave. Equally, what you do – how you behave – can affect how you feel and what you think.

Imagine, for example, that you came home to discover that the shower wasn't working or the heating had broken down. Again. You're angry. Your angry response could have begun with a physical reaction: tense muscles, increased heart rate and rapid breathing. This triggered a behavioural reaction – you thumped the table – followed by the thought. 'Oh no! Not again. I've had enough of this!'

Or, perhaps you thumped the table first which triggered a physical response: your muscles tensed and your heart rate and breathing increased. Again, your thoughts follow close behind.

Or the angry response could begin with the thought 'Oh my God! Not again. I've had enough of this!' This thought triggered an increase in your heart rate, rapid breathing and tensed muscles. And then you thumped the table.

When it comes to emotional intelligence, it helps to be more aware of and understand these different aspects or parts of an emotion.

In Practice

Let's not forget that the little emotions are the great captains of our lives and we obey them without realising it. – Vincent Van Gogh

Each of the situations below has provoked an emotion: anxiety, joy and disappointment. Each emotion has possible physical responses and possible cognitive and behavioural responses.

Imagine what those physical feelings, thoughts and behavioural responses might be for yourself. Could they be different for someone else?

Situation: Giving a presentation at work
Emotion: Anxiety
- Physical feelings:
- Thoughts:
- Behaviour:

Situation: Passing a test, exam or receiving a job offer
Emotion: Joy
- Physical feelings:
- Thoughts:
- Behaviour:

Situation: An event you were looking forward to being cancelled
Emotion: Disappointment
- Physical feelings:
- Thoughts:
- Behaviour:

Next time you experience a strong emotion – for example anger, joy, guilt, embarrassment – try to identify each aspect – the physical feelings, the thoughts and behaviour. Breaking an emotion down into smaller parts makes it easier to see how the different parts are connected, how they interact and how they can affect you and other people when they experience an emotion.

UNDERSTANDING THE POSITIVE INTENT OF EMOTIONS

Never apologize for showing your feelings. When you do, you are apologizing for the truth. – José N. Harris

We often think of emotions as being either positive or negative. But the idea that we should aim to only have 'positive' emotions such as happiness, hope and compassion is not helpful because it suggests that we should try to avoid or suppress 'negative' emotions such as resentment, impatience and jealousy.

The fact is, *all* emotions have a positive purpose. Emotions such as fear, anger, sadness and regret might not feel good but they do have a beneficial purpose.

Fear is a clear example of an emotion that has a positive purpose: to protect you. Anxiety also has a positive purpose. Anxiety about an exam, for example, can motivate you to focus, to cut out all distractions and revise. Anxiety only becomes negative if it so overwhelms you that you're unable to think clearly enough to do the revision.

The problem is, when we experience a 'negative' emotion, we often have a tendency to enforce it with negative responses. Take regret, for example. The positive intent of regret is to prompt you to learn from and avoid making a similar mistake in future. Regret is only negative if you become stuck in negative thoughts, self-blame and inaction. But it's not the emotion that is negative; it's your thinking and lack of action!

In Practice

Your intellect may be confused, but your emotions will never lie to you. – Roger Ebert

Try to keep in mind that emotions serve a positive purpose. Emotions are your mind and body's way of communicating with you. They're trying to get you to take positive, helpful action in response to something that has happened, is happening or could happen.

- What, do you think, might be the positive purpose of guilt; the feeling of responsibility or remorse for some offence or wrongdoing that you believe you've committed?
- What, do you think, might be the positive purpose of anger; the strong feeling, the sense of injustice, in response to the feeling that you or someone else has been wronged?
- What, do you think, might be the positive purpose of envy; feeling resentful because someone else has something you don't?
- What, do you think, might be the positive purpose of disgust; a strong aversion, a feeling of revulsion, nausea or loathing in something or someone?

Be aware that when you ignore, suppress or deny an emotion, when you become overwhelmed or paralysed by an emotion, you prevent yourself from receiving and understanding the positive, helpful information the emotion is trying to convey to you.

UNDERSTANDING HOW EMOTIONS ARE RELATED

Just because you've got the emotional range of a teaspoon doesn't mean we all have. – Hermione Granger

How many emotions do you think we have? Fifty? Eighty? More than a hundred? Some people might claim that there are just six basic emotions – joy, surprise, fear, disgust, anger and sadness – and that all other emotions derive from them.

Of course, there are many, many more emotions besides these six. But are emotions such as envy and jealousy really that different from one another? What about irritation and annoyance – are they the same thing?

It's not easy to distinguish one emotion from another; to tell where one emotion ends or another begins. And when, for example, it comes to emotions like happiness and disappointment, we know from experience that emotions have different levels of intensity; that we can feel very happy or a bit happier, extremely disappointed or only slightly disappointed.

Furthermore, we can also feel more than one emotion at any one time – nervous and excited, sad but relieved – which adds another dimension of complexity to our emotional experience.

To try and understand emotions more clearly, to understand their separate and related qualities and characteristics, psychologists and researchers have attempted to categorise emotions; to show the differences and the relationships between them.

In Practice

There are four basic emotions – mad, sad, glad and scared. And if you touch those emotions then you can grab your audience, your reader. – Larry Winget

Put 'W. Gerrod Parrott's group of emotions' into a search engine. You'll see that Parrott suggests there are six basic emotions and that all other emotions stem from these six basic emotions. For example, both guilt and disappointment stem from the basic, primary emotion of sadness. Pride and relief come from the basic emotion of joy.

Put 'Robert Plutchik's wheel of emotions' into a search engine. You'll see that Plutchik has created a 'wheel of emotions' as a way of categorising emotions and seeing how they are related. The wheel consists of eight basic, primary emotions and eight 'advanced' emotions. Each 'advanced' emotion is made up of two basic ones; for example, contempt is created from anger and disgust. Optimism is a blend of joy and anticipation.

Plutchik's idea is related to a colour wheel; in the same way that primary colours blend to create other colours, primary emotions combine to create a spectrum of human emotions. He suggests that each primary emotion has a polar opposite. For example, surprise is the opposite of anticipation.

Understand emotions; make links. Does Parrott's way of categorising emotions give you a clearer understanding of the intent, motivations and behaviour underlying those emotions? Does it help you to better understand emotions such as remorse and regret, by tracing them back to the basic emotion of sadness. Or jealousy and envy back to the basic emotion of anger?

Does it make sense? Do you agree?

Looking at Plutchik's wheel of emotions, does the combination of sadness and surprise suggest disapproval to you? Is love the combination of joy and trust? Do you think fear is the opposite of anger?

TUNING INTO YOUR INTUITION

Intuition does not come to an unprepared mind. – Albert Einstein

If you've ever experienced the feeling that something in a situation wasn't right, that things didn't seem to add up, then you've experienced intuition. And if you've ever experienced situations where everything did add up and everything did seem to come together, that's also your intuition. It's an immediate knowing. You don't know why, you can't explain it, you just feel it and you just know it.

Intuition is a process that gives you the ability to know something without thinking. It's below the level of your conscious awareness. It's a process that bridges the gap between the conscious and unconscious parts of your mind. It connects emotion and reason.

Your mind and body are constantly picking up information from the world around you. When you get a strong feeling about something, your subconscious brain draws on your past knowledge and experience and remembers a particular set of circumstances – events, actions, behaviour, physical feelings and thoughts, smells, tastes and/or sounds. With lightning speed, it uses this information to warn you not to proceed or tell you that this is the right set of circumstances and to go ahead.

Intuition cuts out all the thought and leaps straight to the answer. It is noticeable enough to be acted on, yet too quick for you to need to process and understand it.

In Practice

Trust your hunches. They're usually based on facts filed away just below the conscious level. – Joyce Brothers

Focus and pay attention! So often, intuitive messages are drowned out by all the other noise and activity that is going on in and around you. When you feel your intuition is speaking to you, ignore distractions and interruptions so that you can tune in to the true feelings, thoughts, words and images that come to your mind.

In any situation, be open to all the messages your intuition is communicating. Be alert for a combination of signals that all seem to add up to the same message. When the combination of messages that your senses are receiving does add up, your intuition will come through loud and clear; everything will instantly come together.

Be more aware of your environment. All your senses are constantly picking up information from the world around you. Being more aware of your environment – the sights, sounds, smells, etc. – on an everyday basis, will alert you when things are different; when things aren't right.

'Listen' to your body and the signals it may be giving you. When something doesn't feel right, or you feel unsure about something, the physical aspect of an emotion will often alert you. Think, for example, about a time when someone tried to persuade you to do something that you really didn't think was the right thing to do. What physical feelings did you experience?

Respect other people's intuition. Show regard and consideration for other people's intuition. When they tell you they 'just know' something but can't explain it, do take them seriously.

UNDERSTANDING NON-VERBAL COMMUNICATION

When the eyes say one thing but the tongue another, a practiced man relies on the language of the first. – Ralph Waldo Emerson

We all communicate information to each other about our needs, feelings, intentions, likes and dislikes, etc., not just by what we say, but by what we don't say. It's usually quite easy to tell when someone else is angry, frightened, surprised, disgusted, joyful or sad – they don't have to say anything, it's usually written all over their face!

But other emotions can be harder to read; you can't just rely on a person's facial expression to tell you how they might be feeling.

Of course, you could ask, but what a person says about how they feel and what they *actually* feel can be two very different things. People aren't always honest or clear about what they're feeling. They do, however, give clues. We all do. Through our non-verbal communication.

According to research carried out by Professor Albert Mehrabian, the communication of emotions and feelings is made up of 7% what is said, 38% tone of voice and 55% body language. This means that 93% of how a person is really feeling is communicated non-verbally.

Facial expressions, posture, gestures and tone of voice are all emotionally driven and can give you clues and provide useful or reliable information about a person's true feelings and intentions.

In Practice

I'm not a mind reader. But I'm reading the signs. – Miley Cyrus

Look for more than one clue. A single expression or gesture won't usually tell you as much as a combination of gestures, posture, facial expression, and tone of voice that a person is displaying. You'll need to look for a *combination* of non-verbal expressions.

You'll also need to take into account the *context* – the particular circumstances or situation that a person is in – when you're trying to interpret how they might be feeling.

It's this combination of non-verbal signals and context in which they occur that gives you a reliable insight into their feelings, intentions and needs.

Unconvinced by what someone is saying? When someone isn't coming across as honest or 'real', when it doesn't ring true or feel right, it's because that particular combination of verbal and non-verbal signals doesn't add up. For example, although a person is all smiles when someone else wins the award, their lack of eye contact and overly bright, high-pitched voice leaks their true sentiments when they offer their congratulations!

Look out for changes. A change in a person's emotions will be evident in their non-verbal behaviour. Whatever is happening on the inside can be reflected on the outside.

Practise your ability to 'read' other people. Observe people interacting with each other in bars, restaurants, cafes, shops and notice how they act and react to each other. Try to guess what they are saying or get a sense of what's going on between them.

Turn down the sound on a TV drama, debate programme or soap opera and observe the gestures, facial expressions, tone of voice, etc. that people display. What combination of non-verbal communications leads you to conclude that a person is expressing a particular emotion?

FINDING THE WORDS
FOR EMOTIONS

Is it really possible to tell someone else what one feels? - Leo Tolstoy,
Anna Karenina

When you say 'I'm happy', what sort of happy are you? Are you 'The sun is shining, it's a lovely day' happy, 'My team just won' happy, or is it more like 'The medical tests are all clear' happy?

Often we're not very clear or even sure about how we're feeling. For example, you may have an experience which leaves you thinking 'I just feel awful!' Awful is not an emotion, but it may be the closest you get to describing how you feel.

Finding the right word or words to explain how you feel isn't always straightforward or easy. And whatever you might mean when you use the word 'happy' to describe how you're feeling, it might not mean the same for someone else. Although the word 'happy' has a buoyant, upbeat meaning for most people, for others, happiness relates to feeling unstressed; that nothing is bothering them. For them, happiness means something different – it has a quiet, calm meaning.

Being able to identify and name emotions more clearly will help you to more easily understand, anticipate and manage feelings and behaviour; your own and other people's.

In Practice

One's vocabulary needs constant fertilising or it will die. – Evelyn Waugh

Notice and name your emotions. Start by just noticing how you feel in different situations. Can you name the emotion that you're feeling? When you feel 'great' or 'awful' see if you can you pinpoint it to a word that more specifically describes the emotion you're feeling.

Take your time. There are a range of situations where you might not be clear about how you feel or your feelings are overwhelming you. Take a minute to think about it; taking time to engage the thinking part of your brain and being aware of how you feel about a particular situation can help you respond in an emotionally intelligent way.

Annoyed, delighted, indifferent. Which words do you often use to describe how you're feeling? Look up the definitions of those words in a dictionary or on a website such as www.dictionary.reference.com. Do you agree with the definitions? Does each definition reflect how you feel when you use those words or would you describe it differently?

Build your emotional vocabulary. Developing your vocabulary of names for feelings can help you to better express emotions. How many emotions can you name? Try going through the alphabet and think of one emotion for each letter.

Put 'emotional vocabulary' into a search engine for a list of words that describe emotions.

Put 'emotions with no English words' into a search engine. Few of us use all – or even most – of the many English-language words available to us for describing our emotions, but even if we did, most of us would still experience feelings for which there are, apparently, no words. In some cases, though, words do exist to describe those nameless emotions – they're just not English words.

OWNING YOUR FEELINGS

No one can make you feel inferior without your consent.
– Eleanor Roosevelt

Being let down by a friend, seeing your partner behave badly at a social occasion or being yelled at because you made a mistake at work. These kinds of situations all have feelings attached to them. How might you feel in any of those situations? Disappointed, embarrassed, upset? Hurt and angry?

And if you want to tell the other person how you felt, what would you say? Would you say 'You embarrassed/hurt/upset me'? 'You made me angry'?

Responding in this way suggests that other people and circumstances are responsible for your emotions. Not so. You create your emotions. And everyone else creates their own emotions.

Blaming someone else can be a way to justify how you feel. You convince yourself that you feel like this because of what the other person did. It's not your fault you feel this way – it's their fault. You don't like feeling like this, so you blame someone else. You take on the role of being a victim, convinced you are suffering through no fault of your own.

Taking full responsibility for your emotions will help you better manage them. Why? When you take responsibility for owning your emotions, then like anything else that belongs to you, they are yours to manage and deal with.

In Practice

Winners take responsibility. Losers blame others. – Brit Hume

Think of the occasions when you have felt guilty, angry, upset, jealous or disappointed. Did you blame someone else for feeling the way you did? At any point did you think or say 'You/he/she/they made me feel …'? In future, try to be more aware of the situations and events when you blame other people and situations for how and what you feel. In any situation where there is difficulty or contention, ask yourself 'How or what do I feel?' and then answer yourself by saying 'I feel …' and not 'He's is making me feel …' or 'She's made me feel …'.

Rephrase what you say. Saying, 'You made me angry' blames the other person for how you feel.

On the other hand, saying, 'I am feeling angry' is taking responsibility for feeling that way.

How could you rephrase the last three sentences, below?

You've embarrassed me … I feel embarrassed
You've been dishonest … I feel deceived
You made me feel I've done something wrong … I feel …
You've disappointed me … I feel …
You've made me feel really small … I feel …

MEETING EMOTIONAL NEEDS

Happiness is an inside job. Don't assign anyone else that much power over your life. – Mandy Hale

Each and every one of us has essential physical and emotional needs. Physical needs are things like food, water, sleep, warmth and shelter. Emotional needs are things such as the need to be accepted, appreciated and believed. To be liked and loved, respected and reassured. To be able to trust and feel trusted. To understand and be understood, to feel valued and worthy.

Each of us differs in the extent to which we need these needs to be met. Just as some of us need more water, more food or more sleep, others may need more freedom and independence, and some of us may need more security and social connections than other people do. One person may need more of a sense of achievement; another may need more acceptance and admiration.

Whatever the level of your emotional needs, when they're met, you're more likely to feel secure, balanced and that your life has purpose and meaning.

But just as we can't blame other people for 'making' us feel bad, we can't rely on others to meet our emotional needs and 'make' us feel good.

It's not that we can't connect with others to help meet our emotional and social needs, it's just that we can't expect them to be solely responsible for meeting those needs.

In Practice

*You would not want to be responsible for someone else's happiness so
please don't make them responsible for yours. – Jennifer O Neil*

Identify your emotional needs. Rather than blaming someone else
for your unmet emotional needs, identifying them can help you take
responsibility for meeting those needs. You already know that hunger
and thirst are signals that you need to do something to meet those
physical needs – you must eat and drink. So, just as you will experience physical discomfort if your physical needs are not met, neglect-
ing emotional needs will result in emotional discomfort.

How do you know if you are emotionally needy? If you often
expect other people – your partner, friends, family or colleagues – to
make you happy. If, for example, you rely on others to keep you from
being bored or lonely. If you constantly look to others for approval
and validation. If you always expect others to show gratitude and
appreciation for things you have done for them and feel let down
when they don't. If you often get upset and usually need someone
else to soothe and comfort you.

Take responsibility for your needs. Just as when you're hungry you
take responsibility for feeding yourself, the same is true for your
emotional needs. Once you have identified a need, do something
about it. If, for example, you're bored, try to create your own interests.
If you are lonely, find ways to connect with other people.

RECOGNISING BELIEFS AND EXPECTATIONS ABOUT EMOTIONS

Denial ain't just a river in Egypt. – Mark Twain

Whether we're aware of it or not, we all hold beliefs about what emotions mean and what would happen if we and other people did or didn't express particular emotions.

As we grew up, many of us learned that to feel and express certain emotions was 'bad' or 'wrong'. Our emotions may have been ignored by others, derided, belittled or denied. This would have done little to teach us about understanding and managing feelings and emotions.

If, for example, you were reprimanded for expressing anger or jealousy when you were younger, you may now attempt to suppress, ignore or deny those feelings when they arise.

You may have learnt that if someone treats you unfairly, it's 'wrong' to hope that something bad happens to them. It's also wrong to be pleased when something bad does happen to them!

You might also have been brought up with the belief and expectation that you have to feel an emotion – love, forgiveness, contrition or guilt – even when you don't feel it.

The problem is, when you have a belief that you 'shouldn't' have a particular emotion, you may try and ignore or suppress it and you cut off the opportunity to understand what the emotion is trying to tell you. And when you feel that you 'should' feel a particular emotion, you can feel guilty or confused that you don't have that feeling.

In Practice

But feelings can't be ignored, no matter how unjust or ungrateful they seem. – Anne Frank

Even though unhelpful beliefs may be rooted in childhood, you can learn to think in a more positive, helpful way about emotions. You can replace unhelpful and disempowering beliefs about emotions with more useful and empowering ones.

Reflect on what you think about situations and associated feelings:

What are your thoughts about feeling and showing – Disappointment? Jealousy? Guilt? Resentment?

Do you feel OK about expressing these emotions? How do you feel when other people show that they feel disappointed, jealous, guilty or resentful?

What are your thoughts and beliefs about – Forgiving? Apologising? Trusting?

What do you feel has to happen before you can forgive someone? If you apologise, do you expect to be forgiven? What needs to happen before you'll trust someone?

Challenge your beliefs. Whatever your thoughts on the emotions listed above, ask yourself 'Why do I think that? In what way is it helpful for me to think like that? In what way is it unhelpful?'

Be curious about other people's beliefs and expectations too. What do you notice that other people say and believe about emotions and expressing emotions? How often do you hear people say 'I know I shouldn't feel like this, but ...'?

Watch how easily children get angry and sad, happy and excited. Notice how the adults around them deal with the child's emotions.

UNDERSTANDING EMOTIONAL TRIGGERS

*Trigger: anything, as an act or event, that serves as a stimulus
and initiates or precipitates a reaction or series of reactions.
– www.dictionary.com*

We all have emotional triggers: specific situations and experiences that provoke an emotional reaction. Pleasant experiences can trigger happy emotions. Certain songs and music, for example, can trigger positive memories of happy occasions and events.

But difficult situations and experiences can trigger difficult emotions.

Something not working on the computer is a trigger for most of us, but often, different events and situations trigger different people. Maybe, for you, it's when someone criticises what you're wearing. It might not be a big deal for someone else, but for you it triggers feelings of humiliation. Maybe you suddenly realise you've forgotten to phone your parents and immediately you're thrust into a bout of anxiety and guilt. Maybe it's someone else's dangerous driving; if someone suddenly pulls out in front of you, for you, it's like a red rag to a bull.

Emotional triggers often lie behind some of our worst behaviour. If you're unaware of your emotional triggers, these negative behaviours can seem automatic and out of your control.

Learning to recognise your own personal trigger situations is the first step to changing your unconscious, automatic reactions.

In Practice

Life is a very emotional experience. – Tony Goldwyn

Identify your triggers. You can't predict every situation but there are some that you know will push your buttons. What can suddenly make you scared and frightened? What immediately frustrates you? What sort of situations always leave you feeling disappointed and resentful? What do you know for certain will leave you feeling embarrassed or humiliated? Write down those situations.

Learn what your triggers are – what makes you angry, jealous, guilty or resentful. Often, you won't identify your trigger until after it's pulled. In future, every time you have an immediate strong emotional reaction to something, write it down. You don't need much detail, just two or three sentences noting the emotion and what happened to trigger the emotion.

Notice your thoughts. 'How dare he!' 'Oh no! I feel awful', for example. The physical feelings: maybe you feel tense, breathe quickly, and you can feel your heart beating. Your behaviour: feeling tearful or raising your voice and snapping at other people.

Be aware of situations that make you more vulnerable to being emotionally triggered. When you're tired, hungry, had too much to drink, stressed, etc. These are times and situations where, when you encounter a trigger, you won't have as much control over your emotions and your outbursts. Until you pay attention, you may never have really noticed that whenever you were hungry, for example, you were more easily triggered.

Be aware of situations you know will trigger a strong emotion. Do any of these situations trigger you? When you're rejected, blamed, judged or criticised? When you feel unwelcome, ignored or rejected or that someone is trying to control you? When you feel a sense of unfairness and uncertainty? Identifying and understanding your triggers is the first step to managing them.

PART 2
MANAGING EMOTIONS

HAVING CONFIDENT BODY LANGUAGE

As the tongue speaketh to the ear so the gesture speaketh to the eye.
– King James 1

When we interact with other people, we're not usually aware of how much we convey, non-verbally. But as research shows, our non-verbal communication often reveals our feelings and emotions far more clearly than what we say.

Our facial expressions, the gestures we make, the way we stand or sit, how fast or how loud we talk and how close we stand to other people all send strong messages about what and how we're feeling. Consciously or not, other people draw conclusions about our attitudes and emotions. And even if we're silent we're still communicating through our posture and facial expressions.

Our body language and non-verbal behaviour play a big part in whether the person we're interacting with feels comfortable. For example, when what you say doesn't appear to match your gestures, facial expressions, etc., your mixed messages create confusion and distrust for the person listening to you.

Being aware of what contributes to helpful non-verbal communication – body language, gestures and so on – can help develop confidence, trust and rapport between you and other people.

In Practice

I speak two languages. Body and English. – Mae West

You can influence how you feel and how you come across to others by simply changing your posture. There's no need to adopt a range of poses, gestures and expressions that feel strange or unnatural to you; you only need to adopt a couple of 'confident' gestures or expressions and the rest of your body and mind will match up.

If you want to feel more capable and confident, not just *appear* confident but genuinely *feel* confident, simply choose to do just two or three of these actions:

- Stand or sit straight.
- Keep your head level.
- Relax your shoulders.
- Spread your weight evenly on both legs (if you are sitting, uncross your legs, putting both feet flat on the floor).
- If you are sitting, keep your elbows on the arms of your chair (rather than tightly against your sides).
- If you are sitting, hold your hands palm down in your lap, or on the table.
- Make appropriate eye contact.
- Lower the pitch of your voice.
- Speak more slowly.

You can't control every aspect of your non-verbal communication; in fact, the harder you try, the more unnatural you will appear. But if you can just use one or two of those actions consistently, your thoughts, feelings and the rest of your behaviour will catch up.

It's a dynamic process; small changes in how you use your body can add up to a big change in how you feel, how you behave and the impact you have on other people.

Which two non-verbal behaviours would you use? Choose two and practise using them in a variety of situations.

DIALLING DOWN
HEIGHTENED EMOTIONS

When it comes to displaying feelings ... you have to be careful. There's passionate, and there's emotionally unstable. – Alexandra Levit

Receiving a rejection letter, your child refusing to eat their dinner, disapproval from your parents, being humiliated in front of a group of people, being asked to work overtime. Again. We all have emotional triggers, specific situations that provoke a strong emotional reaction.

Emotional triggers often lie behind some of our worst behaviour. If you're unaware of your emotional triggers, these negative behaviours can seem automatic and out of your control. But once you're more aware of the sort of situations that you know will trigger strong emotions, you can develop strategies to dial down and manage difficult emotions.

Emergencies aside, most situations need clear, calm thinking rather than blind, emotional responses. Rather than react automatically, you need to be able to stop and think; to access the rational, thinking part of your brain so that you can respond in a conscious, purposeful way – a way that doesn't make things worse.

As soon as you notice that you are reacting emotionally – feeling it in your body: feeling tense, breathing quickly, heart beating – or you notice your behaviour: feeling tearful or raising your voice and snapping at other people – you need to do something to dial it down.

In Practice

Emotions say hurry. Wisdom says wait. – Author unknown

Focus on your breathing. Try this:

- Stop breathing for five seconds (to 'reset' your breath).
- Next, breathe in slowly for three seconds and then breathe out more slowly – for five seconds. Be aware that it's the out breath that will slow everything down.
- Continue focusing on breathing in to a slow count of three and out to a slow count of five, for a minute.

It won't completely dispel the emotion – disappointment, anxiety or frustration – but it can bring you to a calmer place.

Engage your brain. Write a note that says 'STOP! THINK!' and place it on your computer, fridge or somewhere you're likely to see it when you want to avoid saying, or doing, something you'd regret later.

Distract yourself in a way that you know works for you. Go for a five-minute walk. Look at a book or website with beautiful scenery or beautiful art. Listen to beautiful or soothing music. Use sensations, such as holding ice or taking a hot shower, to distract you.

Let it out. Sing to loud music. Shout and scream where no one will hear you.

Take time out. Excusing yourself to go to the bathroom is an acceptable way to have time out without explanation. You can use the time to think about what you're feeling and how you might respond positively.

Think ahead. Intense emotions can blind you to the future. Think about how you will see your reaction tomorrow, in a month's time or in a year's time. How will you feel then?

MANAGING STRESS

*If you ask what is the single most important key to longevity, I would
have to say it is avoiding worry, stress and tension. And if you didn't ask
me, I'd still have to say it. – George Burns*

Stress is the feeling of being under too much mental or emotional
pressure. It's the strain and distress that's caused as a result of being
overloaded with pressure and demands. Stress can affect how you feel,
think, behave and how your body works.

Although most people find that major events such as losing a job, relationship breakdown or money problems are a struggle, it's not just major
life events that are stressful.

Different people find different events and situations more or less stressful than others. We each have a range of events or situations – deadlines,
delays, doing several things at once, catching up with what you haven't
done and what you've yet to do, other peoples' needs and demands –
that are particularly stressful to us.

Most of us might be able to cope with one thing we find stressful, but
when difficult situations and challenges mount up it can become a real
struggle to cope. Feelings of stress overtake your mind and prevent you
from thinking clearly.

You need to calm down the emotional part of your brain and engage
the rational, reasoning part of your brain so that you can work out what
practical things you can do to manage and reduce the stress.

In Practice

For fast-acting relief, try slowing down. – Lily Tomlin

Acknowledge and accept the feeling of being overwhelmed. You may not like what's happening, but instead of fighting it and becoming more stressed and emotional, by recognising and accepting that you're stressed, you can calm your emotional thinking and engage the reasoning, thinking part of your brain.

Slow down. Do everything 20% slower. It might feel weird, but physically slowing down not only gives your brain the opportunity to think and come up with ways to manage the stress, but also, the mere act of slowing down makes you less stressed. Try it!

Get some breathing space. You can do this anywhere at any time. Simply take two or three minutes to stop what you're doing and focus on breathing. A two-minute breathing space will help you to calm down, collect and clarify your thoughts.

Once you can think straight, prioritise; work out what's important, what really needs to be done. Plan what you need to do. Think through the steps you need to take and how you will do them. It's easier to get straight on to the next step if you have already planned what and how you are going to do it. It allows you to maintain a steady pace and keep the pace going. Tell yourself 'I have a plan. I can manage this'.

Give yourself more time. Reduce your commitments and give each commitment more time. Don't plan things close together, instead, leave room between activities and tasks. If you're constantly rushing from one thing to another, give things more time. If you think it only takes you 30 minutes to get somewhere, perhaps give yourself 45 minutes so you can go at a leisurely pace and not get stressed if delays occur on the way.

MANAGING DISAPPOINTMENT

We must accept finite disappointment, but never lose infinite hope.
– Martin Luther King, Jr.

Not being offered the job, the promotion or a place on the course are all sources of disappointment. So are the 'didn't really hit it off' internet date, seeing your team lose, or a New Year's Eve party not being much fun.

Disappointment happens when things don't go the way you hoped or expected that they would. It can leave you feeling let down and discouraged; a natural response to the hurt and sadness that occurs when your expectations or hopes fail to materialise.

And yet any person who has succeeded or achieved something has overcome disappointments. Instead of allowing disappointment to overwhelm or paralyse them, make them cynical or pessimistic, they learned from their disappointments and adjusted their plans so that they could get back on course to achieve what it is that they wanted to achieve.

Emotional intelligence allows you to recognise that disappointment has a positive purpose; it's actually helping you to move towards your goal, not away from it. How come? Disappointment prompts you to reflect on what happened and adjust your expectations. Your experience has resulted in learning something – whether about yourself, another person or the situation – and to move forward with what you have learned.

In Practice

If we will be quiet and ready enough, we shall find compensation in every disappointment. – Henry David Thoreau

Sit with it and feel it. Disappointment is an emotion that's rooted in sadness and, like sadness, when you feel disappointed, you need to sit with it; to take time to acknowledge and accept that what has happened *has* happened. Nothing can change that.

Learn from it. When was the last time that you were disappointed? What did you learn? Did you even stop to reflect on this? Learning from disappointment involves reflecting on what happened, identifying what went wrong, and working out what needs to be adjusted or changed in order to lessen the chance of similar disappointments happening in the future.

Make a decision that you're going to move on. Dwelling on what failed to materialise keeps you stuck and unable to move past the disappointment. All the time you allow your thoughts to brood on what did or didn't happen, all the time you're trapped in negative thoughts, you make it difficult to think and act constructively on your situation.

It won't happen automatically, you have to decide that you *are* going to look for something positive about the situation and think about what can be done. Be open to new ideas and ways of doing things. Rather than thinking 'I should/shouldn't have', try saying 'Next time I'll ...' or 'It might help to ...' or 'I could ...' or 'Now I'm going to ...'

Anticipate future disappointment. Having a back-up plan will not only help you feel secure but will also lessen the disappointment if things don't work out. Supposing, for example, you don't get the job. If you have already applied for other jobs, in case you don't get this one, you've got other job possibilities to think about. As the writer Alain de Botton says, 'One of the best protections against disappointment is to have a lot going on.'

MANAGING REGRET
AND REMORSE

The past is a great place and I don't want to erase it or to regret it, but I don't want to be its prisoner either. – Mick Jagger

Regret arises from thinking that at some point in the past, you made a 'wrong' decision to do or not do something. You blame yourself; you feel a sense of loss and sorrow and wish you could undo a choice that you did or didn't make.

Maybe you regret something you did or said; you regret telling someone what you really thought of them, regret that you took this job, had that last drink or piece of cake. Conversely, you might regret something you *didn't* do or say; such as not telling someone what you thought or how you felt about them, not working harder at school, not taking that job or not finishing a relationship sooner.

Regret is distinct from remorse. Remorse is the regret we feel after we've done something which we deem to be harmful or hurtful to someone else. Times when, for example, we've betrayed a friend or partner or shouted at and berated the kids.

Is there a positive aspect of regret and remorse? Of course! Regret and remorse motivate you to make up for and learn from your mistake and to behave differently in future.

In Practice

Never look back unless you are planning to go that way.
– Henry David Thoreau

Sit with it and feel it. Just as with disappointment and guilt, when you feel regret or remorse you need to sit with it; acknowledge and accept that what's done is done and can't be changed.

Learn from it. Learning from regret and remorse involves reflecting on what happened, identifying what went wrong, and working out what needs to be done next. Look for the lessons. What did you learn about yourself? What did you learn about someone else? Rather than thinking 'I should/shouldn't have ...', try saying 'I should have ... but now I'm going to ...' or 'Next time I'll ...' or 'It might help to...' or 'I could ...' or 'Now I'm going to ...'

Get a sense of perspective. If you regret something, consider the circumstances at the time you did or didn't do that something. Maybe you had no way of knowing what the consequences would be; perhaps you were under pressure to make a quick decision, had other commitments or limited support when you did or said what you did. Be kind to yourself; know that you did what you did with what you knew at the time. Think about what you would say to someone else in the same situation to make them feel better.

Take responsibility. If you feel remorse, take responsibility and ask yourself if there was something else you could have done; an honourable high road you could have taken, instead of the low road that you veered off on? In future, are there some boundaries you need to set and hold yourself accountable to?

Identify and commit to steps you can take now that are proactive. Is there a conversation you need to have? Have you apologised? If for some reason it is not possible to apologise – the other person is no longer around or part of your life – write out your apology, imagine that you have been forgiven. Then move on.

FORGIVING

Forgiveness doesn't require condoning some offensive act, forgetting what happened, or reconciling with the perpetrator, it means finding a way to free oneself from the claws of obsession about the hurt.
– Daniel Goleman

Minor offences such as someone interrupting you, someone pushing in front of you in a queue, or someone knocking a drink over your carpet are relatively easy to forgive and forget. But what if you're faced with more serious issues? What if your friend has seriously let you down, your partner has had an affair, you've been unfairly sacked or you've received an injury as a result of someone else's actions?

Is it possible to forgive and forget? What's the point of forgiving? And what does forgiving actually involve?

Forgiveness is for you and not the other person. Forgiveness means letting go of the resentment, frustration or anger that you feel as a result of someone else's actions. It involves no longer wanting punishment, revenge or compensation.

Forgiving doesn't mean giving in, minimising, excusing or forgetting the offence; the other person is still responsible for their actions. They may not deserve to be forgiven for your pain, sadness and suffering but *you* deserve to be free of this negativity.

In Practice

Forgiveness is almost a selfish act because of its immense benefits to the one who forgives. – Lawana Blackwell

Know that forgiveness is a process. It's not a switch you can flip immediately. Even if you don't have the will to forgive right now, you can still work towards it. Start by acknowledging how you feel. Angry, upset, disappointed? Jealous or resentful? All of these? Even if it's not what you would like to be thinking and feeling, let yourself feel the emotions and process them.

Let go of why. Understanding why someone did something can be helpful, but often, we will never know why someone hurt us. You don't have to know why something happened in order to let go.

Write them a letter that you may or may not send. Say everything you couldn't say to the wrongdoer; how it made you react and how you were affected. Once you're finished, you may find you don't need to say it to them at all, and all you needed to do was get it out.

Decide if you want to give the other person the opportunity to make amends. If the situation allows and if the other person apologises, decide if there's something you'd like them to do to help you trust them again. Although it can help to forgive someone if they are willing to acknowledge the harm they have done and somehow make amends, this doesn't always happen.

Think positive. Think back, for example, to anyone who might have helped and supported you when you suffered the wrongdoing. Thinking in this way – directing your mind to the positive aspects of the event – can help interrupt angry, bitter, resentful thoughts. Keep your mind focused on what's going well in your life, the things that make you happy, and the people in your life who have not wronged you.

MANAGING JEALOUSY

Jealousy is when you worry that someone will take what you have. Envy is wanting what someone else has. – Homer Simpson

When a person feels jealous, they feel that someone or something is threatening something they value. In relationships, jealousy happens between partners, family members, friends and colleagues, when one person thinks that someone or something is coming between them and another person and that they're going to lose out in some way.

A low level of jealousy can be good; it can keep you on your toes and help make sure you're not complacent and taking someone for granted. The positive intention of jealousy is to protect you from losing out – to alert you to the fact that you may need to up your game; make an effort to improve or guard against something or someone slipping away from you.

But with extreme jealousy, it can be easy to see the other person's every act and decision as suspicious in some way. Jealousy is often a unique mix of emotions – fear, anger, resentment, sorrow, betrayal, inadequacy and humiliation. You can feel threatened, insecure and inadequate and become oversensitive, hypervigilant and possessive. But desperate attempts to ensure security only create distance. So how to control jealousy more than it controls you?

In Practice

The jealous are troublesome to others, but a torment to themselves.
– William Penn

Take positive action. Ask yourself: 'What is it I think I'm in danger of losing?' Someone else's time, attention, friendship, love, respect? Jealousy can highlight what you value in your friendships and relationships. Sometimes we need a nudge to remember what's most important and realise we might be about to lose out. So use that feeling as a cue to express and show your appreciation.

Learn to trust. Uncertainty is a part of all relationships. You can't control someone but you can learn to trust them. If you've been betrayed in the past, it's understandable that you feel vulnerable. Try not to let past experiences allow you to believe that it's never safe to trust again. Unless you have evidence that someone is deceiving you, trust them; believe in their integrity and honesty. Focus on the positive aspects of your relationship and your time together.

Talk about it. It's not weak to admit that you feel vulnerable, susceptible to being hurt or fear rejection. If you don't say it, you'll show it, which can mean all kinds of accusations and snooping. Own your feelings. Avoid accusing and blaming the other person. Stick to 'I' statements; rather than saying 'You make me feel ...' say 'I feel worried when ...'.

Use your instincts and intuition as your guide. If there's nothing going on, it shouldn't be a big deal for the other person to talk about it, any more than it would be to discuss what you're having for dinner tonight. If the other person can't talk calmly about your insecurities or you don't feel reassured or you always have to ask to get any information at all, it might be a red flag.

MANAGING ENVY

Envy is the art of counting the other fellow's blessings instead of your own. – Harold Coffin

There's always someone we know who has it better than us. Someone who is more skilled, has more money, more happiness or whose children are cleverer than ours. Maybe you've felt envious because someone else got the opportunity that you had hoped for; the job, the house or the new partner.

Envy can undermine your confidence, leave you feeling inadequate and set off thoughts which turn into resentment and bitterness against others.

Perhaps you torment yourself as you read your friends' and colleagues' social media posts and even scan the show-off posts from people you don't actually know all that well. You compare your situation with theirs and find yours wanting; their strengths highlight your weaknesses. You doubt yourself, your abilities and your achievements.

Envy can make you lose touch with who you are. Comparing yourself with someone else – who they are and what they have – means you can only see what they have got and what you have not.

But there are upsides to envy. Instead of dwelling on what you don't have, envy can motivate and inspire you to improve your situation and to achieve your own goals, not just someone else's.

In Practice

Love looks through a telescope; envy, through a microscope.
– Josh Billings

Acknowledge your envy. The next time you catch yourself resenting what someone else has and feel a sense of hurt combined with entitlement, recognise it for what it is: envy. Be aware that when envy narrows your mind, so that you're focused on what others have, you make it difficult to move forward in a positive way. You're stuck. Stuck in your envy.

Stop comparing. Comparing what you don't have to what others do have will only make you miserable. There will always appear to be people who have it better than you. But remember, we always compare the worst of what we know about ourselves to the best we assume about others.

Accept it. If it's not possible to have what the other person has – they're married to a rock star – accept it. Stop comparing yourself. Instead, focus on what you *do* have and what you *can* achieve.

Use your envy to create a goal. That's emotionally intelligent! If you want it, they probably did too. What might they have done to get what they wanted? Rather than wallow in thoughts such as 'Why have they got it? It's not fair', change your focus. Start planning how you can work towards what it is they've got that you want. This will make you more positive and in control since you are no longer comparing what the other person has with what you haven't – you'll be too busy working towards what you want. You won't have the time or a reason to be envious.

Get some perspective. Any time you feel envious, appreciate what you already have as well as what the person you envy has. Instead of thinking 'It's all right for them, they've got it made', try to see the whole picture. Recognise that the other person may not have everything they want and that they have their problems too.

MANAGING BLAME

Fix the problem, not the blame. – Catherine Pulsifer

Your job, your boss, your partner or your dysfunctional family. The kids, your dog, your neighbour two doors down, the media or the government. How often have you looked for someone or something to blame for a situation you find yourself in? How often is someone else somehow responsible for the problems you're having?

There are a number of emotions around blame: anger, frustration, indignation, resentment and disappointment. There may even be feelings of superiority; a moral indignation where you see yourself as good and the other person as bad, 'You're wrong and I'm right.'

Of course, life does present many difficulties and setbacks and in many cases, it really is someone else's fault. But being in the habit of blaming someone or something else for what goes wrong is to cast yourself in the role of the victim; helpless and disempowered.

When you believe that someone else is responsible for the problem, it's easy to think that they're also responsible for putting things right. But if you can see that they are not the problem, then you can look to yourself for the solution; the power is yours.

In Practice

Blame doesn't empower you. It keeps you stuck in a place you don't want to be because you don't want to make the temporary, but painful, decision to be responsible for the outcome of your own life's happiness. – Shannon L. Alder

Recognise when you're blaming. Whether it's your lack of sleep, your broken-down car, the bad advice your friend gave you that you followed, too often we can get into a habit of blaming without realising we're doing it. Try and be more aware of the times you say things like 'It's not my fault ...', 'It's your fault', 'You made me feel ...', 'I couldn't, because they ...', 'You should have ...', 'It's not fair ...', 'Why did you make me ...?'

Once you start realising you've been trapped by your negative, blaming thoughts, you're free to step out of that trap.

Tell yourself that the other person is not the problem. You can choose to believe the other person or situation is the problem or you can choose to believe that they are not the problem and then you look to yourself for the solution. Each time you let go of your attachment to what went wrong or what should have happened, you're free to move forward.

Take responsibility. Consider the possibility that you somehow contributed to the situation. This doesn't mean no one else played a part; it just means perhaps you did as well. You blame your partner because you're out of milk and they always forget to buy milk. So if you know that they always forget, why rely on them to buy it? Think of a way to remind them or buy it yourself.

Maybe it was and maybe it wasn't someone else's fault. It doesn't matter. What matters is what you learned, what you do now and what you do next time a similar situation presents itself.

MANAGING SADNESS

The word 'happiness' would lose its meaning if it were not balanced by sadness. – Carl Jung

Sadness is the sorrow and distress caused by a loss or failure that you have experienced. When you lose something or someone you love, when you fail to achieve something, when your hopes fail to materialise or a good situation comes to an end, this experience of loss can be felt and expressed as sadness.

Sadness produces particular bodily responses that, instead of giving you energy, as anger does, take energy away from you. Your mind and body slow down, to give you time to take in the loss or failure and accept that what has happened *has* happened and that nothing can change that.

Like all emotions, sadness has a positive purpose. Not only does it slow us down and allow us time to take in and then accept what has happened, it's there to help us adjust – to get used to changed, different circumstances.

Expressions of sadness also convey to others that you are experiencing loss or failure so that they can respond appropriately; give you time and space, comfort and support you.

Avoiding sadness or protecting yourself or someone else from sadness doesn't provide the purpose it evolved for; to reorientate yourself and adjust to the new situation resulting from the loss or failure. Avoidance of sadness is not the way to become happier. Understanding and managing sadness is.

In Practice

Despair is what happens when you fight sadness. Compassion is what happens when you don't. – Susan Piver

Let yourself be sad. It's easy to think 'This isn't a big deal, why am I so sad?' Instead, accept sadness for what it is: a temporary and useful state that can help you adjust to changed, different circumstances.

Cry. As the author Rachel Kelly writes, 'Crying has the power to unify our thoughts, feelings and physical body in a way that is cathartic.'

Write about what's making you feel sad. Put words to it. Or pictures. Or music.

Talk to someone: a friend, therapist, family member. Talk to someone you can trust who is just going to listen and comfort, not try to judge or fix you.

Comfort yourself. Get a massage. Eat healthy comfort food. Take a nap. Wear a favourite piece of clothing. Have a warm bath or a hot shower. Doing things that you enjoy can help you move through sadness, even if you don't initially feel like doing them.

Watch an uplifting film or funny pet videos on YouTube. Listen to uplifting music, music that offers or provides hope and encouragement – ELO's 'Mr Blue Sky' or David Bowie's 'Heroes', for example. Go to www.britishacademyofsoundtherapy.com and find their playlist of the 'World's most relaxing music'.

Give yourself time to adjust. But know that rumination - going over and over your feelings of sadness - hinders recovery. Imagine a future when the sadness you're feeling at this moment will just be a sad memory and when you're ready, work towards that.

MANAGING EMBARRASSMENT

And now I've got to explain the smell that was in there before I went in there. Does that ever happen to you? It's not your fault. You've held your breath, you just wanna get out, and now you open the door and you have to explain, 'Oh! Listen, there's an odour in there and I didn't do it. It's bad.' – Ellen DeGeneres

Embarrassment is the feeling of something improper or ridiculous having happened either to yourself or someone else. An embarrassing episode can leave you feeling awkward, self-conscious and even ashamed of something you or someone else has done.

Whatever has made you feel embarrassed, it's always something that you know that other people are aware of. You're not embarrassed when, for example, you trip up at home alone, only when you do it around others!

There's a reason why we say we're 'dying of embarrassment' – everything in you seems to shut down and time slows to a stop. It's social death! Once you start to feel awkward, the chances are that you'll behave even more awkwardly: laugh anxiously, avoid eye contact, look uncomfortable, bluster or stammer.

It's all very uncomfortable for you, but actually, from a social perspective, showing embarrassment acts as an apology to other people; a sign that you regret what you said or did or that you don't approve and want to distance yourself from what someone else did or said.

In Practice

The rate at which a person can mature is directly proportional to the embarrassment he can tolerate. – Douglas Englebart

Confront the situation. Embarrassment is a sign that you care about the way others see you. But it's not so much what happens but rather how you respond to what happens that can lessen the embarrassment. Of course, like my friend in the pool whose bikini top had come off, you could pretend it hasn't happened. She was embarrassed, but rather than show it, she coolly swam away hoping that no one noticed. They had. A better strategy for resolving awkwardness is to confront it directly.

Stay cool and take responsibility for what you did and for what transpired. You're in this situation, now gracefully work through it. Blaming or shamelessly walking away will not help you. If you did something wrong, acknowledge it and apologise. 'Oh dear, I didn't realise you were his sister.' (You thought the woman was his mum.) 'I'm sorry.' Acknowledging and apologising might feel like adding to your embarrassment but it allows others to comment and maybe even reassure you that it was nothing.

However, if the other person is upset, criticises or laughs at you, don't retaliate by getting overly defensive. Then you really will make the situation even more embarrassing! Instead, apologise. But only once more.

Get some perspective. Laugh at yourself. It might make it easier for you to laugh at someone if you tell the story to a friend who wasn't there. As the comedienne Miranda Hart has said, 'The embarrassment of a situation can, once you are over it, be the funniest time in your life. And I suppose a lot of my comedy comes from painful moments or experiences in life, and you just flip them on their head.'

MANAGING LONELINESS

I'm not afraid to be lonely at the top. – Barry Bonds

There's a difference between being alone and being lonely. To be alone means to be *physically* separated from others; to be *physically* on your own. But with loneliness you feel *emotionally* separate and *emotionally* alone.

Of course, when you're physically alone you may also feel emotionally alone – lonely. But often the cliché is also true; it is possible to feel lonely in a crowd. Even though you may be with other people, you might as well be alone because you feel unconnected from those around you.

While the circumstances that can cause loneliness may be different – moving to a new area or a new job, relationship breakup, bereavement, illness, disability, discrimination and unemployment, being a new parent or a carer – the result is usually the same: you feel sad, detached and isolated and that no one understands.

When you're lonely, it's unlikely you'll remember that emotions serve a positive purpose, since what possible purpose can the loneliness serve? Feelings of loneliness alert you to the fact that your need to connect and belong to like-minded people is not being met. Loneliness can motivate you to take the necessary action that will relieve it.

Don't let the sadness and feelings of loneliness overwhelm you; reach out and make some connections!

In Practice

I never feel lonely if I've got a book – they're like old friends.
Even if you're not reading them over and over again, you know
they are there. – Emilia Fox

Do things that make you feel good. Relationships with other people don't have to be the only way to feel connected; hobbies and interests can also be an important source of stability and connection.

If you have a hobby or interest that you can lose yourself in, you will find yourself actually searching out time to be by yourself in order to do what you really enjoy. Writing, painting, gardening, playing a musical instrument, yoga, running, etc. can help you to feel engaged and connected. Know that periods of time spent alone *can* be rewarding; you can relax and accept a calmer sense of yourself.

Find like-minded people. Whatever you enjoy doing, do it with other people. A helpful place to start is the internet. Look up, for example, local meetups at www.meetup.com which enable you to connect with and meet people in your local community who share your interests. There are groups to fit a wide range of interests and hobbies, plus others you've never thought of.

Join or start a support group. If you are in a specific situation – illness, disability, bereavement – which leaves you feeling isolated and lonely, a support group can offer various forms of help and provide opportunities to share experiences and information. You can get a real sense of connection – feeling that you belong, and are with people who understand you.

Volunteer. Experience the good feelings that come with connecting with – and helping – other people. Search the internet for volunteering opportunities in your area.

Get a pet; a dog or a cat. Aside from companionship, pets can improve your psychological well-being.

MANAGING WORRY
AND ANXIETY

Try not to worry, as it's sticky and hard to scrub off. – Terri Guillemets

We all know what it's like to feel worried and anxious from time to time; to feel fearful at the thought of, for example, an upcoming medical test, job interview or exam. Maybe you've recently been worried about making a speech or a journey, starting a new job or a course at university?

Whatever it is that you're worried or anxious about, you may feel that you've no control over what could happen; how events might turn out and whether or not you'll be able to cope if things do go wrong.

Is there a difference between worry and anxiety? Worry is usually about specific things and relatively short lived. Anxiety may be more or less intense but longer lasting.

Whether it's worry or anxiety you're feeling, you'll experience cognitive, physical and behavioural responses. Maybe your stomach is in knots and you feel nauseous, your breathing is shallow. You may experience 'wired' feelings of tension, be unable to concentrate, fretting and ruminating as negative thoughts dominate your mind.

But, like all emotions, worry and anxiety can have a positive intent; they serve as your internal alarm and prompt you to take the necessary measures to prevent the worst case scenario from happening.

In Practice

Worry is just curdled energy! – Henie Reisinger

Manage the physical feelings: get moving. A brisk walk, running, cycling or climbing a few flights of stairs can use up adrenaline produced by worry and anxiety and be a distraction from worrying thoughts. So can housework – cleaning the bathroom or kitchen, vacuuming, making beds, cleaning windows or gardening. Identify for yourself what sort of physical activities could help you.

Manage your thoughts. Learn to plan instead of worrying. Worry involves your mind going over and over the same problems. A good plan though is more positive:

- Identify what you're actually worried about. What's the worst that can happen?
- Identify possible solutions; what your options are to minimise or manage the worst case scenario.
- After you've decided which option to take, make a plan of action.

Once you have a plan, if you find yourself worrying tell yourself, 'Stop! I have a plan!' and keep your thoughts on that. Visualise a positive outcome – create images for yourself where you see yourself coping and things turning out well.

Manage your behaviour. Switch off from worrying. Listen to music, read a novel, watch a film, do a puzzle – a crossword or sudoku – play a computer game, go out with friends, have a game of tennis. Do some work or housework; anything that makes it difficult for worrying thoughts to find their way into your head.

Talk about it. Voicing your worries can take away a lot of their scariness. If you can't talk to a partner, friend or family member, talk to your doctor and/or call a helpline.

MANAGING ANGER

Get mad, then get over it. – Colin Powell

Whether it's social and political issues or things and people that aren't working as they should, there's a wide variety of situations and other people's behaviour that can 'make' us angry. Anger is a natural reaction to feeling wronged by something or someone; to unfairness, dishonesty, being treated badly, being let down, being lied to or being ignored.

Anger does have positive purposes. If it's justified and expressed appropriately it can be a legitimate way to let others know how strongly you feel about something and it can get you what you want. An angry person is highly motivated to act. As Doreen Lawrence, campaigner and mother of Stephen Lawrence, who was murdered in a racist attack in South East London in 1993 has said, 'The anger has kept me going. Without it I'll crumble.'

Anger can be a useful motivating force, but it can just as easily be destructive and do more harm than good. Often, we either try to suppress it and pretend it's not there or we give full vent to our anger. You can get yourself completely wound up or you can bring yourself down into a calmer place and manage how you express your anger. Even though it doesn't feel like it at the time, you do have a choice.

In Practice

If things go wrong, don't go with them. – Roger Babson

If you're so angry that you can't think straight, then you need to bring those feelings down until they have less of a grip on you and you can engage the rational, reasoning part of your brain.

Learn to recognise your physical signs of anger. Perhaps your voice rises, you feel your breathing increasing and your body gets tense. Maybe your jaw tightens and you feel your heart pounding?

Take some deep breaths. Slow, focused breathing helps bring your heart rate back down; count to three on the in breath and count to five on each out breath. Do this for a couple of minutes. It will also help to engage the thinking, reasoning part of your brain. Just having to think about counting as you breathe will help re-engage your logical thinking brain.

Anger is an energy. – John Lydon

Let off steam. Remove yourself and go somewhere to calm down. Go for a run or brisk walk, a shower or bath, put on some loud heavy rock, scream or swear where it won't alarm anyone. Thump a mattress or pillow. Whatever works for you.

Think about what you do and don't want to happen. Once you've calmed down enough to engage your brain, you can use anger in a constructive way. Think of potential solutions – what do you want to happen next? What will you do if you don't get what you want? Think in terms of consequences and solutions and alternative ways forward, not threats and punishments.

MANAGING GUILT

Guilt is to the spirit what pain is to the body. – Elder David A. Bednar

Guilt comes in all shapes and sizes. You can feel guilty not only for something you did or failed to do, but also for what you think: wishing someone pain, misfortune or even death. You might feel guilty about your feelings – that it's wrong to have felt angry, or jealous or, in certain circumstances, happy. Perhaps you've experienced guilt about not feeling something such as not reciprocating love, or not feeling grief over the death of someone close.

And then there's legitimate guilt and imagined guilt. Legitimate guilt is for something you did actually do wrong and for which you must take responsibility. This type of guilt can be positive; it can motivate you to do something to make up for your wrongdoing. It's not so good, though, if you allow yourself to get stuck in guilt or overcompensate in an attempt to make up for your wrongdoing.

Imagined guilt happens when you feel guilty for events that are not your responsibility; things you cannot control, but for one reason or another, you feel it's your fault. Imagined guilt may arise from feeling responsible for other people's feelings, behaviour and well-being, doing better than someone else, feeling that you didn't do enough to help someone or surviving something that other people did not.

In Practice

Guilt is good for you, provided it lasts no longer than five minutes and it brings about a change in behavior. – Author unknown

Recognise the kind of guilt you have; legitimate or imagined? If, for example, you feel guilty because you bad-mouthed a colleague so that you'll be more likely than them to get the promotion, your guilt is legitimate. If, though, you got the promotion because you were more qualified and experienced and feel guilty anyway, then your guilt is imagined.

Manage legitimate guilt. Without exaggerating or minimising what happened, acknowledge what you did wrong and the hurt the other person is feeling. Address the degree to which you were responsible; there may have been something you could have done differently, but you may not be responsible for everything. Overestimating your responsibility can prolong guilt longer than necessary.

Apologise. Say sorry. Try to avoid justifying what you did or pointing out the parts of the situation that you were not responsible for. Don't complicate it with extra explanations or attempts to revisit the details of the situation.

It's important that you and the other person know that you're aware of the damage done and are clear on what, if anything, you can do to make amends. Make amends as soon as possible, but at a pace that works for them, rather than pushing to fix things fast so as to alleviate your guilt.

Deal with imagined guilt. If your guilt is actually imagined guilt, recognise that blaming yourself for a mistake or incident that was not within your control means that, for some reason, you're sad, upset and even angry at yourself. You're misdirecting those feelings for situations and events that are beyond you.

MANAGING EMOTIONAL EATING AND DRINKING

Physical hunger comes from your stomach. Emotional hunger comes from the head. – Author unknown

Emotional eating is eating – usually 'comfort' or junk foods – in response to emotional feelings instead of physical hunger. Many of us turn to food when difficult feelings arise. It's understandable; eating is a quick way to manage your emotions. You don't like feeling sad, anxious, bored, angry or guilty – you feel like you need chocolate, cake and crisps – and so you're able to comfort or distract yourself immediately.

We often turn to food and drink to feel better and to feel safe. Food can feel like a friend. But eating 'comfort foods' only stuffs down your emotions and leaves your feelings unprocessed – it's a short-term fix – you're still anxious, bored, angry, guilty, sad or upset.

(The Germans have a word – *Kummerspeck* – for the excess weight gained from emotional overeating. Literally, grief bacon.)

Emotional eating often leads to feelings of guilt; you know that you're eating for the 'wrong' reasons; not only have you eaten badly, you feel bad too. It's a vicious circle!

The occasional spell of emotional eating is okay, but the problem is, it can become a habit, preventing you from learning how to resolve emotional distress effectively both now and in the future. Without the ability to manage feelings in helpful ways, you're susceptible not just to emotional eating, but to other unhealthy, potentially harmful behaviour such as drinking, smoking and drug taking.

In Practice

Whatever the problem is, the answer is not in the fridge.
– Author unknown

Identify your triggers. Making yourself more aware of the situations, places or feelings that make you reach for the comfort of food is the first step to managing emotional eating.

Be mindful of what and when you are eating. Emotional hunger often leads to mindless eating. Before you know it, you've eaten a whole pack of biscuits without realising. When you're about to reach for food, instead, before you eat, wait one minute. While you're waiting, ask yourself, how and what are you feeling? Be aware of thoughts going through your mind and what the urge feels like physically. Even if you end up eating, you'll have a better understanding of why you did it and maybe respond differently next time.

Surf the urge. When the urge to eat hits, it's all you can think about. Try surfing the urge. Imagine the urge as a wave in the ocean. It will build in intensity, but soon break and dissolve. Imagine yourself riding the wave, not fighting it but also not giving in to it. Know that cravings aren't permanent, they come, and then they go. Just like the waves.

Don't leave yourself vulnerable to emotional eating. Avoid letting yourself get too hungry or too tired. When your body is hungry or tired, it's less equipped to fight off cravings or urges.

Learn to meet your emotional needs in ways other than eating. Find other ways to reward and comfort yourself besides food (or drink or drugs). Sure, these other ways will not always be as quick and easy at comforting you as food. But a hot shower, a good book or film, yoga, a run or a walk, a chat with a friend about how you're feeling are all healthier for your well-being.

MANAGING CRITICISM

The trouble with most of us is that we'd rather be ruined by praise than saved by criticism. – Norman Vincent Peale

When someone criticises you, how do you respond? If you're like most people, you probably return the attack, or defend yourself or shrink and crumble. There is, though, another option. Accept the criticism, and try to grow from it.

In 2015 Pete Wells, restaurant critic for *The New York Times*, published a harsh criticism of Thomas Keller's award winning New York restaurant 'Per Se'. Wells wrote that the food was 'respectably dull at best to disappointingly flatfooted at worst'. He described the dishes as 'random', 'purposeless', 'rubbery', and 'flavourless'. How did Keller respond? In an open letter to restaurant guests, he accepted responsibility, apologised and promised improvement, stating, 'We believe we can do better for ourselves, our profession and most importantly our guests'.

Of course, it doesn't feel great to be told you're not doing, looking, talking or behaving as someone else thinks you should. Often, someone else's criticism is unfair or even abusive. Fair criticism, though, describes behaviour that can be improved on.

Criticism opens you up to other people's experience and perspective of you – what you think, say and do.

OK, it might not all be accurate and the other person may be harsh and may have exaggerated (especially if they're upset, frustrated or angry), but there still may be seeds of truth in their criticism.

In Practice

Let me never fall into the vulgar mistake of dreaming that I am persecuted whenever I am contradicted. – Ralph Waldo Emerson

Think of a time when someone criticised you. What did they accuse you of? Can you describe in a sentence or two what exactly the criticism was? Be honest, can you now see any truth in that criticism? Are you, for example, harsh or unreliable, untidy or selfish? Was what you said to someone actually mean or insensitive?

Next time someone criticises you, listen carefully. Imagine that someone said 'You're always late. Why don't you let us know or answer your phone? You never think about the people you keep waiting, wondering if and when you're going to turn up. You're selfish.' Could any of it be true?

Even when it's not delivered gently, you have a choice – you can get upset and let emotion overwhelm you or you can put your feelings aside and try to learn from the criticism.

Look for the solution. Don't minimise the problem. Don't sidestep the issue, shift the blame or make excuses. If they haven't said so already, ask the other person what they suggest you do to put things right and improve the situation. (You don't have to agree with their solution though.)

You might agree or disagree that their criticism is valid and agree or disagree with how they want you to rectify the problem. Either way, ask yourself 'What can I learn from the other person's perspective?'

If you honestly feel that their criticism is unfair and invalid, say so. Calmly tell the other person you understand that's their perspective and explain how or why their criticism is unfair or wrong. Or say nothing and let it go. Most likely their mind is already made up and if you try to argue you will just be adding fuel to the fire.

PART 3
DEVELOPING YOUR
EMOTIONAL INTELLIGENCE

PRACTISING POSITIVE THINKING

Positive thinking is not just the feeling you have when good things are happening in your life – when it's easy to feel optimistic. It is about being able to maintain that feeling of hopefulness and motivation, whatever is happening. – Sue Hadfield

Positive thinking is a key part of emotional intelligence. Why? Because emotional intelligence involves managing emotions and situations in a positive, optimistic, helpful way; recognising the positive intent of emotions.

In contrast, negative thinking involves a negative interpretation of events and emotions. Negative thinking focuses on – and often gets stuck in – the difficult aspects of emotions and situations.

Imagine, for example, that you'd promised a colleague you'd complete a report for a presentation she had to give the next day. You get home and realise you'd forgotten to complete it. Now you're worried. You feel guilty. You tell yourself that you're hopeless. Instead of acknowledging the mistake and then thinking what positive action you can take, you're mired in negative thoughts, self-recrimination and blame. 'I'm hopeless. Why can't I remember to do things? She should've asked me earlier; given me more notice. Why do *I* have to do all the last minute work?'

Allowing the negative thinking that goes with mistakes, difficulties and disappointments to overwhelm you only serves to stop you from moving forward. But with emotional intelligence, you can acknowledge the difficulties and then move on to responding in positive, constructive ways.

In Practice

Things turn out best for the people who make the best of the way things turn out. – John Wooden

Try to be more aware of the way you think. More often than not, you won't even notice when you're thinking in negative ways. Think of an event or experience that often happens to you – delays to a journey you often make, colleagues, clients or a family member who you find difficult to get on with, particular chores or aspects of your work that you don't like doing. What negative thoughts do you have in those situations?

Now ask yourself, 'What's a positive way of thinking about this?' Once you're more aware of negative thoughts, you can choose whether to dwell on them or move on to positive, encouraging and empowering thoughts. Let's say you catch yourself saying, 'I'm fed up with this cold, rainy weather. It's July! Are we ever going to get a proper summer!' Sure, that's a valid complaint. What's helpful about it? It might prompt you to book a cheap flight to somewhere sunny in September so you've got something to look forward to. That's helpful. But if you stay stuck in complaining about the bad weather, it's not helpful.

Add the word 'but'. Any time you catch yourself saying a negative sentence, add the word 'but'. This prompts you to follow up with a positive sentence.' ... *but* we've still got a couple of months of summer left – there's still time for some lovely hot weather.' And in the case of forgetting to complete the report,' ... but still, I can go into work early tomorrow and get it finished.' Imagine positive outcomes; focus on what you are able to do and what's within your control.

MANAGING CHANGE

It is not the strongest of the species that survive, nor the most intelligent, but the one most responsive to change. – Charles Darwin

The seasons, the weather, the temperature, the price of stamps and interest rates. Changes happen around us every day and we take many of them in our stride. Yet there are many situations at work and in our personal lives – a staff reshuffle or changes in policies and procedure at work, redundancy, moving somewhere new, children leaving home, holiday flights delayed – which, when they occur, interrupt our flow.

Very often, we find it difficult to adapt to changing circumstances. Change – uncertain, unanticipated or unpredictable situations – often brings a range of uncomfortable emotions; worry, anxiety, confusion, uncertainty, resentment and fear.

Emotional intelligence involves understanding and managing the emotions that come with change. It's not so much what changes happen that matters, but how you respond to them.

Emotional intelligence supports effective responses to change; it encourages you to acknowledge and accept uncertainty while at the same time being open to new ideas and new ways of doing things – learning technologies, and procedures, different ways of doing things, working with different people – adapting to changing conditions and adjusting to different roles and responsibilities.

In Practice

If you don't like something change it; if you can't change it, change the way you think about it. – Mary Engelbreit

Write a list of all the negative things, such as uncertainty, that you think change brings. It's important to acknowledge the negative aspects – don't suppress or deny the challenges and difficult emotions that changes bring. Then write down all the positive things, such as new opportunities, that change brings. What feelings accompany these positive thoughts?

Practise making changes. Change is not as difficult as you might think. It's letting go that is hard! Doing something new makes it easier to let go of old ways, provided the new behaviour is constantly repeated. You can easily see this for yourself if you try this; move the clock or the wastepaper bin to a different place in the room. See how long it takes you to stop looking in the wrong place for the time or throwing rubbish on the floor.

Make a conscious effort to maintain flexibility and adapt to change. Choosing to break a routine way of doing things on a regular basis can be an effective tactic for coping with the inevitable changes that you will encounter in your life. What could you do? Take a new route to work or drive a different route to somewhere you walk or drive to regularly? Perhaps you could regularly cook new recipes and try different types of food. Try listening to different radio shows and if you regularly watch a soap opera, switch to a different one for the next few weeks.

Decide to do things differently to experience different results. What new things could you do? Start today. Get used to being flexible and able to change. Know that whenever you are able to adapt, you create the possibilities that don't depend on perfect conditions.

HAVING COURAGE

Courage is not the absence of fear, but rather the judgement that something else is more important than fear. – Ambrose Redmoon

Courage. It doesn't mean not being afraid. Courage means doing something despite your fear. Fear and courage go together. Whenever you're courageous, you're overcoming fear. To overcome fear you need courage. Courage is strength in the face of fear.

When we're frightened of doing something, it's because we're anticipating that something unpleasant will occur. But so often, avoiding fears can make them stronger and scarier; you can spend more time and energy avoiding what you fear than facing your fears and dealing with them. Whether it's courage to do and say things or courage to feel things – to feel emotions such as sadness, envy, disappointment, anger, etc. – if you can accept those fears, let them inform you of what you need to do to prepare yourself, and then work past them.

The people we often admire the most are not fearless. They're courageous; they're good at listening to and then moving through their fear. They have the courage of their convictions, they act according to their beliefs, in spite of their own fears and especially in spite of other people's objections or disapproval.

You can do the same. You can have courage – that brief moment, a pivotal instant in which you take action – act on your convictions, beliefs, instincts and intentions and do what you know is right.

In Practice

Sometimes the biggest act of courage is a small one. – Lauren Raffo

Focus on the positive. Think of how you'll benefit from using your courage – what you'll achieve and how good you'll feel. Knowing *why* you're going to do something can lift your spirits and give you the surge of motivation you need to take the necessary first step.

Plan what you're going to do or say. There's no need to do this in detail, simply think through what you probably need to do – the steps you'll need to take. Visualise yourself successfully doing or saying it.

Don't overthink it. The more you ruminate about whether you should or shouldn't and the longer you have to come up with excuses, the more time you'll have to get yourself scared.

Courage can be prone to leaking, which means the longer you wait, the less of it you'll have. So, once you've decided to do something – talking to your boss about problems at work, confronting noisy neighbours or picking up a spider – don't wait – act. Don't aim to be truly fearless, just act as if you're feeling brave and confident.

Focus on the first step. Having thought through the steps, now just focus on that first step; on saying, for example, 'We need to talk' rather than on worrying about how the talk will go. So often, taking the first step is half the battle, so pushing yourself over the threshold will create the momentum that will move things forward – and by then you'll just be dealing with it.

Build your courage; choose to do something slightly scary. Write down five things that make you uncomfortable. It might include doing something new or going somewhere you've never been before. Or it might be to speak up and say what's in your heart. Do one of these at a time – feel the fear and then do it.

KEEPING AN OPEN MIND: BEING CURIOUS

We don't see things as they are, we see things as we are. – Anais Nin

Children are known for their curiosity. They're interested in the world around them and are full of questions. 'Why is the sky blue?', 'Why doesn't the moon fall down?', 'How do I know that I'm real and not just a dream of someone else?', 'Why do I have two eyes if I can only see one thing?'

Their enthusiasm and curiosity appear to be endless and yet for most of us, for some reason or another, as we grow up our curiosity seems to dry up.

We need to be more curious!

Being curious means being eager to learn or know. Being curious is an opportunity to change what you think and how you view the world.

When you're curious your mind is open and actively looks for new ideas and perspectives. It takes a curious mind to look beneath the surface and discover these new worlds, opportunities and possibilities. Curious people ask questions and search for answers in their own minds and from the minds of others.

Too often, we only understand things from our own perspective but we can develop our ability to seek to understand things differently.

And of course, seeking and trying to understand other perspectives is an important part of developing a crucial emotional intelligence skill: empathy.

In Practice

I would rather have a mind opened by wonder than one closed by belief. – Gerry Spence

Be curious. In a range of situations, make a point of asking how, why, what and when. How might things be different or thought of differently? Wonder and find out about others. Without interrogating, in conversations ask questions such as 'What do you think? Why? How do you feel about ... Why?' and 'Tell me more.'

Do something new. Start saying 'yes' to new experiences. If a friend invites you to go on a hike, say yes. Do a charity walk, run, or bike ride. Try new things, with no expectation other than to feel what they're like. Take something you already do and do it differently. If you go to a yoga class – try a different type – Hatha Yoga, Hot Yoga or Iyengar Yoga.

Read widely. Read autobiographies, read magazines, newspapers and blogs written by people with a different point of view to you – different political or religious views, for example. Read arguments from the other side to see what other people are saying.

Join a book club. It could open you to a wide variety of literature and opinions. Also, after you've read a book, read the reviews on Amazon. Do other people feel differently from you about the book you've just read?

What would Beyoncé do? Ask how Beyoncé, David Beckham, your best friend, your boss, your brother or sister, someone you know to be different to you, might approach a situation or problem you're currently experiencing.

Volunteer. Volunteer your time to work with people whose lives and situations are completely different from yours – elderly people, underprivileged children, homeless people, refugees and migrants.

Keep an open mind. Be open to learn, unlearn and relearn. Some things you know and believe might have a different explanation and you should be prepared to accept this possibility and change your mind.

DEVELOPING PATIENCE

Patience is not the ability to wait but how you act while you're waiting.
– Joyce Meyer

Most days there are plenty of good reasons to be impatient. The queue is moving at a snail's pace. Or you're *still* waiting for someone to send you some information you need, return an email or finish their long-winded presentation. Or it's your children; they're taking forever to get ready.

Whatever it is, you can feel yourself getting agitated, irritated and frustrated. We suffer impatience when we realise that something we need or want is going to take longer than we want it to and we start looking for people to blame and/or ways to hurry things up.

Expressing frustrations as part of an effort to resolve those frustrations and get things done is a good thing, but it needs to be done from a non-irritable, non-hostile place. If not, you'll put others on the defensive. Impatience works against you when you become so stressed you can't think clearly; you can't judge whether it's worth the wait or if you should hurry things along, change course or give up.

Patience, on the other hand, enables you to take a step back so that you can think clearly in frustrating circumstances, stay calm and centred, and avoid acting rashly out of anxiety or irritation. Patience gives you the power of being able to wait, watch and know when to act.

In Practice

You can learn many things from children. How much patience you have, for instance. – Franklin P. Jones

Recognise the physical feelings – tense, fidgeting and restless – that go along with your thoughts that something or someone is taking too long. Can you feel yourself becoming agitated, irritated and frustrated?

Stop fuelling your impatience with how wrong it all is, how slow they are. Instead, tell yourself 'This is merely uncomfortable, not intolerable. I can handle it'. If things do need speeding up, you need to be able to think clearly in order to work out a way forward.

Practise patience. Find a long, slow-moving line to wait in; a traffic jam, supermarket, bank or post office. Instead of getting irritated, tell yourself 'I'm going to wait peacefully'. Look around you; see what there is to see, observe and watch. Act as if you're calm – by acting patient, you can often feel more patient.

Plan for impatience. Whether it's queues, travel delays, people turning up late, learn to keep your mind occupied while you wait. If you can distract yourself – fill in time – you also gain a measure of control. Read. Text or phone a friend. Listen to music or a podcast.

Have patience with other people. People who are physically slower than you or slower at expressing themselves. Remind yourself that your impatience rarely gets others to move faster. In fact, it can interfere with their ability to think clearly and act quickly and competently. All you're doing is creating stress for them.

DEVELOPING WILLPOWER

The first step to becoming is to will it. – Mother Teresa

Willpower involves your ability to do what you intended to do even when you don't feel like it. Willpower is linked to motivation. Motivation involves having a reason for wanting to do something. Willpower gives you the power to keep at it. Your motivation for losing weight or stopping smoking, for example, could be for health reasons. Willpower helps you to keep at it and resist the temptation to give in.

We've all got good intentions – to improve our health, to stop eating junk food, to stay calm in the face of provocation – are just a few examples of when we might need willpower. But if you're like many of us, so often, you struggle to stick with those good intentions and give up or give in. You've lost both your will and your power!

How does this happen?

Your good intentions and will come from the rational, reasoning part of your brain – the part that thinks through what's good for you. When emotions take over, feelings of deprivation and frustration can undermine your intentions and convince you that it's easier to give in and let go.

Developing your willpower helps you to stick with your good intentions, it can help you override the impulsive behaviour that sabotages those intentions. In other words, willpower helps you do what's best for you!

In Practice

Impulsiveness can be charming but deliberation can have an appeal, as well. – Sarah Dessen

Identify and understand the emotion. When you feel that you want to give in or give up, ask yourself 'What do I feel right now? Deprived? Irritated? Resentful? Impatient?' Willpower concerns an inner battle for control. Instead of fighting these feelings, acknowledge and accept them. Then remind yourself of the reasons *why* you want to do something.

Surf the urge. When the urge to give in happens it's all you can think about. Try surfing the urge. Imagine the urge as a wave in the ocean. Imagine yourself riding the wave, not fighting it but also not giving in to it. And if you do surf the urge, reflect back on having done so and feel good about yourself for having conquered it.

Distract yourself and avoid thinking about what's tempting you to give in. Redirect your attention; focus on your breathing, do a few simple exercises or get up and go for a walk. Read, watch something or play a game on a screen. Be prepared; have distractions that you know work for you so they're ready to hand when temptation strikes.

The idea is that the more your mind and body are tied up in other actions, the less your mind reverts to thoughts of giving up and giving in.

Plan for times you know you might be low on willpower. For example, if you're trying to cut down on alcohol, don't arrange to meet friends for drinks on a day that you know is going to be difficult at work.

MAKING DECISIONS

I make all my own decisions. And I take full responsibility. – Kanye West

How do you make the right choice, know that what you choose will work out, and if it doesn't, that you won't regret having made a different decision? Quite simply, you don't, can't and won't. You can never know for sure when you make a decision that it's going to turn out well.

Whether it's choosing to eat Mexican or Indian, deciding to stick with this job or change jobs, knowing if you should to tell someone what you really think or keep quiet, or whether to pay that unreasonable parking fine or fight it – often, your instinct and emotion is pushing you to go one way, but your rational thinking is telling you to consider the pros and cons and consequences of a decision and go in a different direction.

If you go with what feels right you may worry that you're being too impulsive and could miss out on a 'better' option. And yet overthinking can lead to confusion and obscure what you instinctively feel is the right path to take.

It's not easy or necessary to separate the emotion out of a decision; making a decision requires both emotion and reasoning. The key to confident decision making is to balance your emotional reactions with your logical responses.

In Practice

It's not hard to make decisions when you know what your values are.
– Roy Disney

Know how emotions can influence the choices you make. Emotions like pride, guilt, resentment, anger, joy, relief and love can inform or impede decision-making abilities. Become more aware of emotional triggers – the circumstances and events that provoke a strong reaction and prompt you to make a decision that you may later regret. It's not using your emotional intelligence if, for example, you've had a delayed, frustrating commute to work and the emotions you felt on the train influence the decisions you make at work that morning. If what you're feeling is something unrelated to the decision, try not make the decision right away. Only pay attention to those feelings that are relevant to the decisions being made.

Use your head. In any given situation, identify what's important in the situation and what you're hoping to achieve. This focuses your mind and narrows your choices so that you pay attention to relevant factors, not irrelevant ones.

Trust your intuition. When you do feel strongly that a particular path or choice is the right one, know that it's because your decision is in line with your aims and values.

Accept uncertainty; make a choice despite possible unknowns. For the times when you feel uncertain, know there is no 'right' or 'wrong' decision. Instead, ask yourself 'What's the worst that can happen? How might I deal with that?' If possible, have a back-up plan and know that if things don't work out, if and when that time comes, you can deal with it then.

Own your decisions. Whether you chose this restaurant or that restaurant, this job or career or that job or career, if it didn't work out, take responsibility. Don't wallow in guilt, regret or blame. Instead, think about what you learned from that situation that you can use to inform a similar decision, next time.

ACCEPTING

God grant me the serenity to accept the things I cannot change, the courage to change the things I can, and the wisdom to know the difference. – Reinhold Niebuhr

Swimmers who are caught in a rip tide and feel themselves being dragged out to sea often panic and try to swim against the current. Typically, they use up all their energy, exhaust themselves, get a cramp and drown. The advice to swimmers in this situation is not to resist, but instead, accept the situation, and let the current take them out to sea. Within a few hundred meters the current will weaken and the swimmer can swim around and back to shore.

It's the same with emotions: it's not easy to deal with situations and emotions that are challenging and difficult, but resisting is futile – it gets you nowhere fast.

When it comes to emotional intelligence, acceptance means simply feeling whatever you feel without trying to resist or control those feelings. This doesn't mean that you can't do anything about how you're feeling; you don't have to resign yourself to something or give in. Acceptance means understanding that, right now, you *are* feeling irritated, disappointed, embarrassed or whatever it is you're feeling.

Acceptance allows you to understand that any time you deny or resist an emotion, just as a swimmer resists the current, you're spending time and energy that could be better spent in more helpful ways.

In Practice

Once we accept our limits, we go beyond them. – Albert Einstein

Start out by accepting the feelings that go with the small things. Things such as irritation at running out of milk just when you're looking forward to a cup of tea, disappointment at a TV programme being cancelled, feeling envious of a friend's holiday plans. Instead of judging yourself or suppressing your feelings, acknowledge what has happened and how you feel. If you can acknowledge and accept how you feel about the smaller things in everyday life, you'll then be better placed to manage the stronger feelings that come with a missed opportunity, sudden change in plans or a serious provocation.

Allow yourself to feel annoyed, upset, disappointed, etc. about what's happened. Perhaps you're so angry and upset with your bullying colleague, obstinate ex-partner or manipulative parent, you wish they would fall off a cliff. If you then feel guilty about your murderous thoughts, hate and anger, then, on top of feeling angry, you've added the extra pain of guilt.

Avoiding or denying how you feel doesn't help either – it traps you in a constant vigilance against the feeling you're trying to ignore.

Rather than spend your energy pushing the emotions away or feeling bad about having them, when you accept the upset and anger – when you're willing to experience what you're feeling and thinking – you're giving yourself a chance to learn how to manage that feeling.

And, each time you do accept and experience particular feelings, you learn, make it easier and use much less energy than an ongoing, usually unsuccessful attempt to avoid them. Once you've acknowledged and accepted and allowed yourself to feel that, then let that emotion inform a positive, constructive way forward.

ESTABLISHING
BOUNDARIES AND LIMITS

Get this through your head: you are not responsible for other people's happiness. – Bryant McGill

Boundaries are the limits we set for ourselves. Physical boundaries involve our personal space, how close we stand or sit next to someone; whether we shake hands or exchange hugs, for example.

Emotional boundaries are the limits of your emotional abilities, in relation to other people's emotional needs and demands. Setting emotional boundaries involves taking responsibility for your own actions and emotions. Emotional boundaries also prevent you from accepting blame or responsibility for how someone else feels. Emotional boundaries help protect you from feeling guilty for someone else's feelings or problems. They help you avoid, for example, feeling the need to make up for someone's disappointments, soothe their anger or make them happy.

Emotional boundaries allow us to protect ourselves from being caught up in or being manipulated by other people's emotions.

Establishing and maintaining emotional boundaries is not about turning your empathy off; you can still try to imagine, understand and identify with how someone else feels – you just don't have to feel responsible. You don't have to perform some sort of emotional rescue; free or deliver them from their feelings.

Healthy boundaries are flexible though; they allow you to get emotionally involved when it's appropriate and to step back and maintain a distance when one or both of you recognise that the other person has to take responsibility for their own emotions.

In Practice

You teach people how to treat you by what you allow, what you stop and what you reinforce. – Tony Gaskins

Recognise when your emotional boundaries are weak. This might be when you feel overly affected by someone else's moods – your moping teenage son or your anxious friend, for example. Or it could be when you drop what you're doing or need in order to accommodate their immediate emotional needs; a needy family member, for example. Or it might be when you become overly involved in someone else's emotional problems or difficulties such as a colleague going through a breakup.

Set limits. What are you willing and unwilling to accept in terms of other people's emotional needs, demands and behaviour? In a variety of situations, you need to know how far is too far. It doesn't mean that you should cut yourself off, but if you don't know what your limits are, how can you know if you're being flexible or just being a doormat?

Boundaries are not meant to punish, but are for your well-being and protection. They're more effective when you're calm, firm and assertive.

Stop trying to carry out an emotional rescue. Ask yourself 'Do I feel like I just *have* to step in? Or is it something they can do and work out for themselves?' Trust and respect other people to identify, experience and express their emotions in their own way. You can still be involved; be there to support in times of difficulty and celebrate with them when things are going well.

Visualise it. Imagine a line or a fence being the limit of how far you'll go. Or visualise and hear the hinges creaking as your boundary door closes.

When you notice that you're over-identifying with another person and their emotion, turn your attention back to you. You can do this very simply by pinching yourself, shaking your head or your hands or taking deep breaths.

ASSERTING WHAT YOU WANT

What you allow is what will continue. – Author unknown

The builder, plumber or electrician you hired hasn't finished the work they agreed to do. You lent something to a friend and after they returned it you realise it's damaged. You're out for dinner but the meal is not exactly what you ordered. You're working on a project at work which, for a number of reasons, has been delayed and your manager won't give you more time to complete it. And to cap it all, the kids have left the living room in chaos.

Are there similar situations where you didn't assert what you wanted and ended up angry and unhappy because of it? Do you need to learn to be assertive?

Both assertiveness and emotional intelligence involve being able to identify, manage and appropriately express your feelings in direct, honest and appropriate ways. Being assertive means identifying what you do and don't want and saying so clearly and honestly, while at the same time taking into consideration the other person's feelings, needs and wants.

In fact, when you're assertive you encourage others to be open and honest about their views and feelings. This helps develop mutual understanding, empathy and respect. And that's emotionally intelligent!

In Practice

Stay strong. Stand up. Have a voice. – Shawn Johnson

Start by noticing how you feel about the situation. Irritated? Impatient? Anxious? Rather than ignore your feelings and do nothing or let your feelings take over the situation, let your feelings inform the situation. Then you can respond in an assertive, emotionally intelligent way.

Before you say anything, decide three things:

Firstly, what exactly it is that you do or don't want. See if you can say it in just one or two sentences. Any more than that and you're probably going to be waffling or ranting. So, you might say, for example, 'I'd like you to get the trousers I lent you mended and dry cleaned'.

Secondly, decide how far you're prepared to negotiate and compromise. Decide what might be an alternative that works for you and benefits the other person as well. This way, you've neither given in nor insisted that yours is the only way. However, if you do choose to negotiate or compromise, bend as far as you can, but no further. Know what your limits are and stand your ground.

Thirdly, decide what you'll do if you don't get what you want. This is not about threats and punishments. Threats increase the emotional temperature and make an argument more likely. Instead, think about solutions. When you see things in terms of possible solutions, you are looking for a specific answer to a situation.

Ask yourself 'What do I want to accomplish here? A punishment or a solution? Am I prepared to negotiate and compromise?'

Thinking these things through will help you stay calm and in control, knowing you have already planned an alternative way forward.

BUILDING CONFIDENCE

Success comes in cans, not can'ts. – Author unknown

Confidence is not about what you can or can't do. It's what you *think and believe* you can or can't do.

Confidence – self-confidence – is believing that you can do things. When you're feeling confident you have a positive attitude towards yourself and your abilities and you believe that events and experiences are likely to turn out well. Conversely, when you don't feel confident, you're likely to believe that things will turn out badly. You may even feel that there's no point in trying.

When challenges and setbacks occur, if you're feeling confident, you're able to work towards overcoming the difficulties, whereas when you lack confidence you're likely to feel discouraged and give up.

If you don't believe in yourself and your abilities, in a range of situations, you risk feeling bad about yourself; you have low self-esteem. And that just undermines your confidence further and you feel bad again. It's a negative dynamic.

Building your confidence helps you feel good about yourself. And if you feel good about yourself you feel more confident about your abilities. It's a positive dynamic that can also help develop your emotional intelligence. Why? Because when you feel confident, you're more willing to experience and understand emotions and believe that you *can* positively manage them.

In Practice

When you have confidence, you can have a lot of fun. And when you have fun, you can do amazing things. – Joe Namath

Start from a position of strength. Put the words 'positive qualities' into a search engine. Find five words that describe you. Then write a couple of sentences for each word, describing how you know you are, for example, patient, reliable, caring, fun and open-minded. Make these your own personal, positive affirmations; truths about yourself that you *can* believe and feel good things about yourself.

Do more of what you enjoy. What do you like doing? Are there activities in your life that bring you a sense of satisfaction and make you feel good about yourself and your abilities? Whatever those activities are, do them more often. It could be, for example, something to do with your job, voluntary work, a hobby or interest, family and friends.

Build your confidence. Do one small thing every day that scares you just a little and feel your confidence and courage grow.

Identify something you'd like to feel more confident about and take small steps to achieve it. Although it may present a challenge it shouldn't be too difficult. For example, you might like extra confidence to speak up more at work. You could therefore decide, 'I'll just ask one question in this afternoon's meeting'. Make it even easier for yourself; ask a nice person.

Have a clear mental video image of yourself acting in a confident way in a situation where you want to be more confident, as if you were the character in a play. See yourself acting calmly and self-assured.

Keep a journal of each step you take towards building your confidence. With each step write a sentence or two about how you felt and how you think it may have contributed towards your confidence.

ACTING 'AS IF'

Act as if though what you do makes a difference. It does.
– William James

Is it possible to make yourself feel any one particular emotion? Is it possible, for example, to make yourself feel compassionate, interested, confident, motivated or happy? Yes, it is. By acting 'as if'.

Emotions have three aspects: thoughts, behaviour and physical feelings. Any one of these aspects of an emotion can trigger another. This means that what you think can influence what you do and how you physically feel. It also means that your behaviour – what you do – can influence how and what you think and feel.

You can use this to your advantage; act 'as if' and you're on your way to feeling how you'd like to feel.

Chen is a freelance illustrator. He says, 'I know that "feeling like it" rarely comes before actually doing something. So, although I don't feel like it, I push through that feeling, I get started and before I know it, I'm absorbed in drawing. That's what gets me started – knowing that I will feel like it if I just get started'.

As Sir Isaac Newton discovered, objects at rest tend to stay at rest. But objects in motion tend to stay in motion. This is just as true for feelings as it is for falling apples! When you act 'as if', you generate the physical motions, which in turn can trigger the thoughts which correspond to that physical action.

In Practice

If you want a quality, act as if you already had it. – William James

Commit to just five minutes of positive action. Whatever it is you want to feel, spend a minute or two thinking through how you would be behaving if you were naturally feeling that feeling. What would you be saying, doing and thinking? Imagine that you had to sit through a dull, tedious meeting or presentation. You're bored. How can you make yourself feel interested and engaged? Do what you would do if you *were* interested; take notes, ask questions, look interested, ask others' opinions, think about how what they're saying relates to other issues.

Decide what is the one thing you'll do first. Do that one thing. Start doing something immediately, without thinking any further and giving your mind time to resist. Once you start doing something, it's easier to continue doing it. Take action and things will flow from there.

Need to have a difficult conversation with someone? Decide on your opening lines and then jump right in. The conversation will go on from there – it may go well or it may not, but at least you've opened up communication. Want to lift your mood and feel a bit happier? Smile, watch or listen to something you know will probably amuse you, listen to upbeat music, do something you enjoy.

Know that it's a positive feedback loop. Acting 'as if' positively influences further thoughts and actions. Don't wait for your thoughts and feelings to change to take the action. After a short time, the feelings which you would like in a particular situation will start to emerge naturally.

Try it – with no expectation other than to see what it feels like.

PART 4

DEVELOPING YOUR
SOCIAL INTELLIGENCE

LISTENING FOR FEELINGS

If speaking is silver, then listening is gold. – Turkish proverb

Contrary to what you may think, listening is not a passive process, it's an active process. You need to put aside distractions and pay attention in order to really understand what someone is saying and what they really mean. And when it comes to emotional intelligence, as well as listening to someone tell you what they think, what they've done or are going to do, etc., you need to be listening out for feelings.

Imagine, for example, that a friend has told you a long story about his manager's unreasonable behaviour. If you've been listening closely, your response might be, 'It sounds like you felt humiliated by your boss. I get a sense that you feel she's undermined you once too often.'

He might reply, 'Yes I was humiliated – you're right – she's done this once too often!' Or he might clarify his thoughts and feelings and respond with, 'Humiliated? No, actually it was more than that – I was furious! But yes, undermined *is* what I've been feeling.'

Either way, by listening and trying to understand what the other person is feeling as well as saying, you show that you're trying to see things from their point of view. You're being empathic.

In Practice

What differentiates us from animals is the fact that we can listen to other people's dreams, fears, joys, sorrows, desires and defeats – and they in turn can listen to ours. – Henning Mankell

Confirm your understanding. In situations when emotions are running high, you can get confused. It can be helpful to restate part of what you've heard. You may start off with 'So I am right in thinking ...' or 'Can I just be clear ...?'

In fact, getting into a habit of listening *as if* you were going to repeat back (as you do when you're listening to someone give you directions) is a really good way to train yourself to focus your thoughts on listening.

Watch and listen. Be aware of the connections between verbal and non-verbal communication. Do they all 'say' the same thing? Ask the other person, for example: 'You said you understood, but you look unsure. Can you tell me what you're feeling about it?'

Ask open-ended questions. How often do you ask people about their feelings with questions which demand 'yes' or 'no' answers? For example, 'Are you OK with this?', 'Are you upset?', 'Are you happy now?' These closed questions mean that the other person really only has two possible responses – 'yes' or 'no' – and it's likely that they will not say any more about how they feel. Instead, ask open-ended questions such as 'How do you feel about that?'

Practise listening for feelings with a friend. One of you talks for two minutes on one of the following subjects:

- The best or worst job you ever had
- The best or worst holiday you ever had.

When the speaker has finished, the listener should summarise what the speaker said; repeat in your own words your understanding of what the other person said. What were the main points of what they said? What feelings were apparent?

EMPATHISING

The great gift of human beings is that we have the power of empathy. – Meryl Streep

Empathy is the natural ability that we all have to understand how and what someone else might be experiencing, thinking or feeling from within the other person's frame of reference. It involves trying to recognise and understand the meaning, significance and implications of someone else's experience, thoughts and feelings, even when they differ from your own.

In the context of emotional intelligence, when you're being empathic, you're aiming to understand the other person's emotions; how they feel about a particular situation.

If there are similarities between you and the other person in background or experience, you might assume you know what they're feeling. You may have had the same experience, but empathy means understanding another person's unique, subjective experience. You draw on your own understanding and experience of emotions and feelings to help relate to what others are saying and feeling, but keep in mind that the other person might feel or think differently than you do in any given situation.

In Practice

Could a greater miracle take place than for us to look through each other's eyes for an instant? – Henry David Thoreau

Just listen. Whether it's about you or not – the other person might, for example, be annoyed that they've just received a parking ticket or they might be upset with you because you advised them it was OK to park there – do nothing but simply listen and accept what they are saying and feeling.

You might not agree with how they're feeling, but accepting how the other person feels goes a long way to validating the other person's emotions. So don't interrupt, don't try to fix it, pacify them, offer solutions or stop their experience or expression of what they are feeling. First, just listen.

What to say? Empathy isn't necessarily knowing exactly what someone is going through or how someone feels; it's getting that you might not get it. And even if you totally don't get it, you get that it's hard. Or that it's not fair or confusing or upsetting or whatever it is the other person is feeling.

The simplest gesture – a gentle touch, a sympathetic look or a thumbs up – can often convey empathy without words.

When you do say something, don't say 'I know how you feel'. Do say something like 'I'm sorry that happened ... It must be hard/confusing/annoying/disappointing/upsetting for you'. In this way, you're validating that whatever it is, you understand that for them, it is hard, difficult, upsetting or confusing.

MANAGING SOMEONE'S DISAPPOINTMENT

I really don't know how this company would survive without you,
but from Monday, I thought we'd give it a try and find out.
– Author unknown

It's a cruel joke, but telling someone they're not in the team, that they've not passed the test or got the job, whatever it is, letting someone down or giving someone bad news is not a joke – it's never a pleasant thing to have to do.

Often, it can be just as hard for the person giving the disappointing news as it is for the person receiving it. There are two issues: firstly, knowing when, how and what to say and secondly, managing the other person's reaction; their disappointment, tears and/or anger.

While you shouldn't have to change what you want to say completely to suit another person's needs, thinking of the situation from the other person's perspective can help you say what you want to say in the best way, while handling hurt feelings.

In Practice

The price of being close to the President is delivering bad news.
You fail him if you don't tell him the truth. Others won't do it.
– Donald Rumsfeld

If you can, prepare what you're going to say. It's also helpful to anticipate the reaction and questions the other person might have. However, if you need to give the news right away, you can say 'I need to talk with you about...'. This at least gives them some warning instead of you just blurting out the news.

Explain why. Briefly explain what's led to the situation. Setting the context – the circumstances relevant to the issue – can make a difference to how bad news is grasped and understood. For example, 'We've thought through who we want on the team. Each and every one of you has the potential and skill. We're not selecting just on individual strengths, it's also how each player fits in with our tactical plans'. After you've set the context, state the bad news simply and honestly. 'I'm sorry but you won't be playing in the league final'.

Acknowledge their emotions. Unless the disappointment affects you directly too, don't make their situation your own and get too emotional yourself. Your response should reflect your understanding of how the other person feels. 'I'm sorry you're so upset. I can see this makes things difficult/is disappointing for you'.

Do not say 'I know just how you feel', or 'Try not to worry about it'. Although you might mean well, the other person may feel that you actually *don't* understand or that you're just trying to move off the subject.

Say what, if anything, you can do to help. Suggest possible actions or ideas on what steps to take next. Focus on what can be done rather than what can't be done. If you don't have the answers to any of their questions, say so. If you know where they can get information that might help to answer their questions, say so.

BEING KIND AND CONSIDERATE

People will forget what you said, people will forget what you did, but people will never forget how you made them feel. – Maya Angelou

Kindness and compassion are two of the most positive qualities of emotional intelligence. Each is rooted in thoughtfulness and consideration – a deliberate awareness or regard for the feelings and circumstances of other people.

Being kind and considerate means looking beyond yourself and making the time and effort to think about how others might be feeling and to be aware and notice how your behaviour can make a positive impact. You make a point of looking for opportunities when you could help someone out. You use your head and your heart to be thoughtful and take action; do something to show goodwill towards others.

Although kindness and consideration expect no reward or recognition, being aware of and doing something to benefit someone else can make both you and the person you are helping feel good. When you think about how to reach out to someone else, you're considering things from someone else's perspective. This can help you to develop empathy.

In Practice

Being considerate of others will take you and your children further in life than any college or professional degree. – Marian Wright Edelman

Anticipate what others might need. Meeting a friend and know that it's going to rain? Bring an extra umbrella. See that a colleague is bogged down with work that day? Fetch him a coffee.

Be considerate of others when you're in public. Keep your voice at a slightly lower than normal level when you're talking on your phone. Let another driver merge (safely) into your line of traffic. Be kind and compassionate to people you don't know – a harassed looking parent, a tired commuter – give them a smile and a kind word.

Think of who in your life could benefit from compassion. Someone who is lonely, unwell or worried about something. Don't feel you have to rescue the other person or make their situation your own. Just make a thoughtful gesture of kindness and consideration; a phone call, a text, bring some flowers or meet for coffee.

Be considerate of other people's financial situations. If a friend or colleague doesn't have much money, don't suggest that you go out to an expensive restaurant, for a night out, holiday, hen or stag do. Unless it's your treat, find inexpensive things to do.

Don't monopolise conversations. Be aware of how much you are talking as opposed to everyone else. The next time you're with other people, be sure you give them a chance to talk. Ask what they think and how they're feeling. It's not all about you!

Be punctual. One of the most inconsiderate things you can do is to act like your time is more important than someone else's. You may not be doing this intentionally, but if you show up late – especially if you make a habit of it – then you're showing you have no consideration for their time or feelings.

MANAGING SOMEONE ELSE'S ANGER

Anger blows out the lamp of the mind. – Robert G. Ingersoll

How many times have you had to deal with an angry person? Perhaps you work in a job where a customer or client was unhappy with the service they received, or a supplier was upset because of a late payment. Maybe a friend has been angry that the information you gave them turned out to be wrong. Or your partner became annoyed because you failed to do something you agreed you would do.

People get angry when the expectations and beliefs they have about a situation and the way things 'should' be differ from what actually happens. If they see this as a negative thing, they will feel wronged, offended, threatened or attacked in some way. They may feel they've been ignored, embarrassed or humiliated, misled or lied to.

The part of the brain that's triggered when strong emotions arise is different from the part that operates in rational and reasonable ways. This means that when someone is angry, it's easy for them to be unreasonable and illogical because the anger has taken over their rational mind. Their ability to think in a clear, calm way has been switched off. It's as if a wall has come down and they are behind it.

It can be really difficult to manage your own feelings; but there are ways to avoid reacting emotionally to someone else's anger.

In Practice

Never go to bed mad. Stay up and fight. – Phyllis Diller

Listen. An angry person needs to let it all out so don't say anything until they have finished. Listen without interrupting because the moment that you dispute what they're saying, it can make them feel even angrier than they are already.

Be clear about what, specifically, the other person is angry about. If there's any doubt, clarify by asking, for example: 'Are you annoyed because you got a parking ticket or because I thought it was OK for you to park here?' At this point you are simply making sure you've understood the situation.

Find out what their expectations are. Ask what they would like to happen now or next time in a similar situation.

Stay calm, speak slowly and use non-threatening language and body language. State how you feel and how you see the situation. You might disagree with their perspective and what they expected. But, you may agree with their point of view. If their anger is directed at you, apologise and explain what you can do to put things right.

Only take responsibility for your own actions. You're not responsible for anyone else's behaviour or for the emotions someone else is feeling. You didn't 'make' them angry. You're not to blame if they choose to be angry or upset with you, someone or something else. They need to manage their own feelings and reactions.

Leave. Do not remain with the other person if they're so angry that they're confusing or scaring you; if they are being abusive or threatening. Say 'I know you're angry but I'm getting confused/scared.' If you feel threatened by an angry person, trust your judgement. Leave if you feel unsafe, or if you're too upset to try and resolve the situation.

MOTIVATING AND INSPIRING

Our chief want is someone who will inspire us to be what we know we could be. – Ralph Waldo Emerson

A friend tells you they'd like to join you on the 10 km run but they're not sure they're fit enough. A colleague wants to apply for a promotion but tells you 'There's no point applying, I probably don't have enough experience'. A family member says they'd like to book a singles holiday but they worry that they'll feel shy and awkward and not get on with the other people on the holiday.

If you want to encourage people to do something, you need to motivate them; give them a reason to achieve something. You'll need to engage their logical, rational, reasoning side. If you want to inspire them, you'll need to spark their soul and light up their spirit. You'll need to engage their emotions and imagination.

Often, in any one situation, you'll need to do both; to motivate and inspire.

Motivating and inspiring other people gives you the opportunity to bring out the best in other people; to tap into people's best intentions and encourage them to believe 'You *can* do it!'

In Practice

Who is going to have the most motivated, most inspired voters show up to vote? You know the answer to this question. – Michael Moore

Find out what motivates people. It could be different from what *you* think ought to be motivating to them, so ask questions. What reasons, what incentives, what rewards do they need in return for their time and effort? Whatever their reasons, if you know of any other benefits, tell them. Maybe it's a financial or material gain. Perhaps it's personal gain; they'll improve themselves or their situation in some way. Whatever it is, tell them and remind them of it.

Acknowledge the challenges, but emphasise the positive. If people are unsure or resistant, find out what their feelings and concerns are. Inspiring others means you acknowledge the difficulties but are clear that they *can* overcome difficulties and succeed. Be positive and optimistic.

Discuss what qualities and strengths they have that will help solve problems and contribute to overcoming difficulties. If you can support people and encourage them when things are difficult, you'll be inspiring them to see the best in themselves and the situation.

Connect emotionally with them. Inspiration requires and involves emotion. What inspires people is feeling excited and passionate about being able to achieve in areas that are important to them. They are inspired by emotions and values like love, anger, pride, justice and triumph. Influence the way people think and feel so that they feel lit up and compelled to take positive actions.

Get them to visualise what success will look and feel like. When you're inspiring people, you're aiming to engage their imaginations and emotions; to get them to feel and see what's possible. Aim to describe things in a way that will generate images in their minds that provide a clear picture of what they're aiming for.

MAKING COMPROMISES

Let's build bridges, not walls. – Martin Luther King, Jr.

Which side of the family to spend Christmas with, where to go on holiday, what colour to decorate the room, what time to leave the party, how to do a particular job at work. We're often faced with decisions that require a compromise.

There are a variety of situations when negotiating a compromise is the best way forward; when a situation requires a quick decision, for example, or when splitting the difference is the fair and best solution to a potential deadlock, or when the importance of maintaining relationships is more important than the outcome of the disagreement.

Of course, each person wants to achieve the best possible outcome for their position, but each person needs to be prepared to modify their demands and accept that they can get something of what they want but not all of what they want. They each need to agree to disagree and live with the decision.

The most important thing for each person involved in a negotiation is that they feel their feelings and views have been considered by the other person and that any decisions or outcomes have come about through mutual understanding and adjustments from both people involved.

In Practice

Learn the wisdom of compromise for it's better to bend a little than to break. – Jane Wells

Think it through. Decide in advance what you want or need, what you're willing to compromise on, what you're less willing to compromise on, and on what issue you will stand your ground.

State what it is that you do and don't want and how you feel. Explain why you want what it is that you're proposing and what the benefits of it are. Then listen to what the other person wants and doesn't want and how they feel. The other person must know they're being listened to and that you understand why their needs are important to them. So find out their reasons and acknowledge their feelings and perspective.

Have a range of outcomes that are open for consideration. Offer more than one possible compromise; several different options that you're willing to work on with the other person. For example, if you're trying to compromise between wanting to decorate the room grey when the other person wants to paint it blue, you could either come up with a third colour that you both like or one person gets to choose the colour for that room and the other person chooses the colour for another room. Or one person chooses the colour and the other person gets to choose the furniture.

Focus on what's achieved. Both people involved need to be aware that the outcome might be less than they had originally wanted. The final decision may be one that is acceptable but not optimal. People can be reluctant or resist compromise as an approach to resolving a situation if the result seems like a loss. Focus on what is achieved, rather than on what has been given up and it's more likely that both of you will be satisfied.

DELEGATING

You can do anything but you can't do everything. – David Allen

Have you ever struggled with organising other people to do their share of the housework, a social event or a project at work? Unsuccessful attempts at delegation in the past can often leave you feeling that it's more trouble than it's worth. Next time, you tell yourself, it will be easier and quicker to do it yourself than explain, guide or cajole someone else.

Perhaps though, when it comes to getting things done you like to take full control – to take all the responsibility and all the credit for achieving something. Or you feel that you'd appear weak and incompetent if you asked for help.

But trying to do everything yourself is not always the best use of your time, skills or energy. It can leave you feeling overwhelmed, anxious and stressed. There's no shame in handing over to someone else; by drawing on their time, skills, knowledge and experience you *can* get things done through other people.

Done well, not only does delegation allow you to make the best use of yours and other people's time and skills, it can help them feel connected, included and involved. And that's emotionally intelligent!

In Practice

Surround yourself with the best people you can find, delegate authority and don't interfere. – Ronald Reagan

Choose the right task for the right person. Unless you've got the time to show someone or train them to do something, be sure that what you're asking them to do matches their ability. People are less likely to resist if it's not difficult. But if you *can* make the time to explain, show or train others to do specific tasks, you develop their skills and abilities. Then, the next time a similar situation comes along you can delegate the task.

Avoid dumping. Often, what you think passes for delegation feels to the other person like dumping. Consider the other person's situation. Do they have time? If so, what do they think and how do they feel about doing what you've asked? Encourage them to decide what tasks are to be delegated to them and when. What are their concerns? Ask them. Then listen to the response. Be aware of their non-verbal communication; what's that telling you about how they really feel?

Motivate the other person. State the benefit; what's in it for the other person. For example, 'If you could do that, I'll be able to get this completed today, then tomorrow we'll both be able to go home early.' Don't patronise. Be positive and sincere – no emotional blackmail. Don't manipulate people with low level threats of how badly either you or they will feel if they don't cooperate!

Follow-up. See if they're OK and need any further support. Be available to answer questions but don't micro manage. Let people do things their own way; this creates trust.

Express your appreciation. Then they'll know that their efforts have been acknowledged and they will be more likely to help out next time.

UNDERSTANDING AND
MANAGING GROUP DYNAMICS

Alone we can do so little; together we can do so much. – Helen Keller

Whether it's a meeting at work, in a classroom or a social occasion, when there are three or more people with a common reason to be together then those people can be considered a group. And whether that group is made up of three people or 30 people, they're each going to have their own individual temperament, quirks and characteristics and they will each take on distinct roles and behaviours when they're in a group.

'Group dynamics' is the term for the effects of these roles and behaviours on other group members and the group as a whole. A group's dynamic is the force that impacts on the motivation, development or stability of a group. It's characterised by forces of personality, ambition, energy and ideas.

In a group with a positive dynamic, individuals work towards collective decisions, they trust and encourage one another, and take responsibility for making positive things happen.

But in a group with poor group dynamics, the behaviour of one or more of the group can be disruptive. Separate individuals could be overly critical or negative of others' ideas. Emotions can often run high; some individuals could be full of enthusiasm while others are sarcastic or appear uninterested.

Dealing with different personalities and personal agendas are common challenges at work and in social situations. It helps to manage the dynamics if you can be more aware of what's going on between people.

In Practice

Never doubt that a small group of thoughtful people could change the world. Indeed, it's the only thing that ever has. – Margaret Mead

Practise people watching. In a variety of situations, observe people and notice how they act and react to each other. Try to get a sense of what is going on between them. Observe how the group interacts. Be aware of how different individuals interact with each other – how they behave differently with one person compared to another.

Be aware of non-verbal communication. What's that telling you about how they really feel? What **combination** of non-verbal language – the gestures, facial expressions, tone of voice, etc. a lead you to conclude that a person is feeling a particular way about the group or other individuals in the group?

Be aware of 'matching and mirroring'. People who are in tune with each other 'mirror' each other; they tend to use the same posture and body language. These are natural signs of a shared liking, harmony and understanding. Look for how other people do or don't mirror each other.

Remind people of what you have in common. When individuals' different quirks, characteristics and agendas appear to be creating poor group dynamics, find a way to remind them why you're together – what you all have in common and what you're all aiming for.

Focus on communication. Open communication is central to good dynamics. Find out how people feel. Ask people not just what they think about issues, problems and achievements, but how they feel.

SHUTTING SOMEONE UP. NICELY.

It's good to shut up sometimes. – Marcel Marceau

Ever been stuck with someone who repeats the same stories and anecdotes or talks about topics in needless detail? Or someone who always manages to bring the conversation back to themselves; complains and moans or brags and boasts?

We all know people who talk without listening, who seem to think that what they have to say is as interesting to everyone else as it is to them and who don't seem to understand that listening is an important part of communicating and connecting to others. People who talk too much not only seem unable to get this balance, they also fail to recognise the often bored, frustrated, resentful reactions and responses of their listeners.

Typically, you the listener get so bored, you either stop listening altogether or you get so irritated and frustrated, your resentment builds and you react harshly and rudely.

Can you take back the reins of the conversation without feeling and appearing rude? Yes. There *are* ways to do it nicely.

In Practice

If a person feels he can't communicate, the least he can do is shut up about it. – Tom Lehrer

Rather than switch off, listen closely. You need to be ready for your opportunity to interrupt. If you listen closely you can pick up on what they've said and then take the subject in a different direction or bring the 'conversation' to a close.

Be ready to jump in. Make eye contact and say their name. If it's appropriate, briefly touch their arm. Stand up if you were sitting down. Or, indicate that you'd like to speak by holding up a hand. When the other person takes a breath or in the brief moment when they finish a sentence, interrupt by saying in a firm but calm tone, 'I'd like to say something ...' or 'I'm just going to interrupt...'.

Add some experience of your own that will confirm that you've listened to what they've told you. For example, 'Well Natalie, your Italian holiday sounds so interesting ...' and before she can say anything else, change the subject. Just go straight into it without drawing breath' ... I've not been to Italy but I've been to Spain and ...' and take the conversation where you want it to go. If you want to get away, just continue by saying 'Well, I've got to get on now ...'

Widen the circle. If you're in a group, try directing questions to someone else. Say 'What do you think of this, Tom?' Or 'Natalie, do come with me. I want to introduce you to Tom/go to the bar/get some food.' This tactic makes them feel included and gives you the chance to take your leave.

Be nice. You'll feel OK about ending the conversation and the other person will feel happier to let you go if you say something positive. 'Thanks, you've given me some good advice about travelling by train in Italy!'

MANAGING THE
SILENT TREATMENT

That arctic blast you're feeling? It's the chill coming off my cold shoulder.
– Michele Jaffe

Is someone giving you the silent treatment? Are they maintaining a distance and keeping conversations with you to the bare minimum? Whether it's your partner, a family member, friend or colleague, whoever it is, it can leave you feeling upset and frustrated. What's going on and why are they giving you the cold shoulder?

By cutting you off, non-talkers can take control of the relationship and the situation. If they feel hurt by something you've done or said, by ignoring you, they can punish you by causing *you* hurt and pain. And because they feel wronged, they might feel vulnerable so it makes sense to them to cut off communication and build a wall of silence so you can't hurt them again. In other words, they're protecting themselves.

Whatever the reason for cutting you off – to control the situation, protect themselves or punish you – how to confront the person who's ignoring you without making things worse?

Sometimes, it's not about you at all. Perhaps the other person is withdrawn because of work or personal problems. In that case, tell them you've noticed they're withdrawn and ask if everything is OK and if there's anything you can do to help.

But if you notice that this person is only quiet or sullen around you and not towards others, then you need to break the ice.

In Practice

Go ahead and give me the silent treatment. Quite frankly I look forward to the peace and quiet. – Author unknown

What did you do? Did you do something wrong or behave badly? Was it something you said? Maybe you accused them of something or turned down a request for help. Maybe you're not sure if you have done or said something insensitive. Ask. You can say 'I feel like there's a problem between us and that you might be upset with me.' But if you do know what happened between you, try asking 'How are you feeling now, about what happened between us?'

Acknowledge what they say about how they feel and then say how you feel. For example, 'I feel sad/bad about what happened.' Or 'I feel guilty for what I did.' Tell them that you want to work things through but be careful not to find fault or lay blame.

Speak in a neutral voice. Make sure your tone doesn't imply they are being oversensitive, overreacting or being ridiculous. A dismissive or patronising tone will only make things worse.

Take responsibility and apologise. This doesn't mean taking all the blame or suggesting that it's completely your fault, it simply means admitting what you did and that you're sorry it happened.

Explain what you can do to put things right. You could, for example, say 'I know that I let you down. I'm sorry. Can I make up for it by ... ?'

What if they still won't communicate? Try only once. After you've apologised and attempted to understand what's going on, you've done your part. Now, it is up to the other person. You can't fix this without their cooperation. Maybe they need time to think through what happened between you, so give them some space.

GIVING CRITICISM

Criticism is the disapproval of people, not for having faults, but for having faults different from your own. – Author unknown

Think back to the last time you criticised someone. Did it go well? Nobody likes being told that they're behaving, acting, looking or saying things the wrong way, but just because people don't like being criticised, doesn't mean you shouldn't.

Criticism can be justified if the other person has failed to do something or has done it wrong or incorrectly. Criticism can be valid feedback – a response from you that can result in change or improvement in the other person's actions.

Often, if you don't speak up, if you hold back the criticism, if you suppress your irritation and frustration, your resentment can build up and can leak out in other ways. And that's not emotionally intelligent.

Is it possible to criticise others without hurting their feelings or making them angry? Thinking in terms of criticism might not be the most helpful approach. Rather than thinking in terms of what someone's done wrong, think in terms of what they can do right. Instead of criticising, which is rarely taken well, offer a specific, positive suggestion.

In Practice

Choose your words carefully. Words are weapons that can be used against you or for you. – Rita Barnes

Think first. Before you say anything, decide what, exactly, it is that the other person has done that's a problem for you. Secondly, decide what change or improvement you want to see. You're the one with the problem – what's the solution? Don't just dump your criticism on the other person, think about what change or improvement you want to see.

Consider, for example, this criticism 'You've gone ahead with the work before I agreed to it. It's not right, it's not what I wanted. You've done it all wrong.'

Constructive criticism describes what can be changed or improved. A better approach would be 'I see you've been getting on with the work. There are a few aspects that I need you to go back over.' And then say exactly what those aspects are.

Choose your words carefully. The right words make the difference. Instead of saying they're 'incompetent' you could tell your colleague they 'could be more careful' and then explain how. Saying 'It would be good if ...' or 'One thing that could help is ...' helps to keep it positive.

Do not accuse. Do not tell the other person '*You* do this and *you* do that'. Instead, use 'I' statements. For example, instead of 'You need to ...' say 'I would like you to...'. Don't be afraid to tell the other person how you feel. 'I was upset/embarrassed/furious when ...' but try to avoid speaking in a tone that's sarcastic, hostile or condescending. Speak in a calm, neutral way. This can make a big difference. Even if you feel the person deserves your anger or sarcasm, it will not help to criticise them in this way. If you do, they will most definitely not respond well!

ABOUT THE AUTHOR

Gill Hasson is a teacher, trainer and writer. She has 20 years' experience in the area of personal development. Her expertise is in the areas of confidence and self-esteem, communication skills, assertiveness and resilience.

Gill delivers teaching and training for educational organisations, voluntary and business organisations and the public sector.

Gill is the author of the bestselling *Mindfulness* and *Emotional Intelligence* plus other books on the subjects of dealing with difficult people, resilience, communication skills and assertiveness.

Gill's particular interest and motivation is in helping people to realise their potential, to live their best life! You can contact Gill via her website www.gillhasson.co.uk or email her at gillhasson@btinternet.com.

MORE QUOTES

Follow your heart but take your brain with you. – Alfred Adler

Feelings are much like waves, we can't stop them from coming but we can choose which one to surf. – Jonatan Mårtensson

Each one of us makes his own weather, determines the colour of the skies in the emotional universe which he inhabits. – Bishop Fulton J. Sheen

When dealing with people, remember you are not dealing with creatures of logic, but creatures of emotion. – Dale Carnegie

Emotions like loneliness, envy, and guilt have an important role to play in a happy life; they're big, flashing signs that something needs to change. – Gretchen Rubin

Criticism may not be agreeable, but it is necessary. It fulfils the same function as pain in the human body. It calls attention to an unhealthy state of things. – Winston Churchill

Unexpressed emotions will never die. They will come forth later in uglier ways. – Sigmund Freud

To carry a grudge is like being stung to death by one bee. – William H. Walton

One ought to hold on to one's heart; for if one lets it go, one soon loses control of the head too. – Friedrich Nietzsche

Poetry is when an emotion has found its thought and the thought has found words. – Robert Frost

I'm not too articulate when it comes to explaining how I feel about things. But my music does it for me, it really does. – David Bowie

All emotion is involuntary when genuine. – Mark Twain

Today you are You, that is truer than true. There is no one alive who is Youer than You. – Dr Seuss

USEFUL WEBSITES

Mental health:

MIND
Phone: 0300 123 3393
www.mind.org.uk
Sane
Phone: 0300 304 7000
www.sane.org.uk

Despair:

Samaritans
Phone: 116 123
www.samaritans.org

Anxiety:

AnxietyUK
Phone: 08444 775 774
www.anxietyuk.org.uk

Relationships:

Relate
Phone: 0300 100 1234
www.relate.org.uk

Bullying:

Bullyinguk
Phone: 0808 800 2222
www.bullying.co.uk

Bereavement:

Cruse Bereavement Care
Phone: 0844 477 9400
www.crusebereavementcare.org.uk

Eating disorders:

Beat
Phone: 0845 634 1414 (adults) or 0345 634 7650 (for under-25s)
www.b-eat.co.uk